CARIBBE/
ODYSSE'

AUSTRALIA AND CRICKET
IN THE WEST INDIES

CARIBBEAN ODYSSEY

AUSTRALIA AND CRICKET
IN THE WEST INDIES

TEXT BY MIKE COWARD
PHOTOGRAPHS BY MICHAEL RAYNER

SIMON & SCHUSTER

AUSTRALIA

DEDICATION

For Earle, Chay, Bibi and Sherwin and the other children of the West Indies who made the odyssey so pleasurable.

CARIBBEAN ODYSSEY

First published in Australasia in 1991 by
Simon & Schuster Australia
20 Barcoo Street, East Roseville NSW 2069

A Paramount Communications Company
Sydney New York London Toronto Tokyo Singapore

© Text Mike Coward 1991
© Photographs Michael Rayner 1991

National Library of Australia
Cataloguing in Publication data

Coward, Mike.
Caribbean odyssey.

Includes index.
ISBN 0 7318 0232 2.

1. Cricket – West Indies. 2. Cricket Tournaments – West Indies.
3. Cricket – Australia. I. Title.

796.35865

Designed by Jack Jagtenberg
Map artwork by Greg Campbell Design
Typeset in Australia by Asset Typesetting Pty Ltd
Produced by Mandarin Offset in Hong Kong

Front cover: Richie Richardson, Man of the Series and arguably the world's finest batsman in 1991, sharing the limelight with Geoff Marsh, who engineered Australia's success in the limited overs competition.
Back cover: A passionate sentiment is expressed in this advertisement outside Queen's Park Oval, Port of Spain, Trinidad.
Page 1: A countenance to light the way in Kingston.
Page 2: Act of faith. Curtly Ambrose and a personal statement.
Page 6: The infectious smile of the Caribbean.

FOREWORD

Just how much rivalry exists between Australian and West Indian cricketers must be obvious to everyone after the last battle for the Frank Worrell Trophy.

But while there was a good deal of controversy and a lot was said in the heat of the moment, I'm sure the incidents won't take away the respect the players have for each other. Certainly I hope no one bears any grudges. Test cricket is particularly hard when you are playing for what many people thought was the championship of the world.

Cricket means so much to West Indian people everywhere. The success of the cricket team makes them feel proud. For many reasons the West Indies cannot afford to fail so there is always a lot of pressure on the team.

Both directly and indirectly Australia has played a big part in the development of the high level of professionalism for which West Indies cricket is now well known. From Keith Miller and Ray Lindwall to Ian Chappell and Allan Border, West Indians have always admired Australian cricketers and followed them with interest. I can still remember the pain of losing 5-1 in Australia in 1975-76 and the shock of playing against such tough opponents. Some of that toughness has rubbed off and the West Indies cricketers are not easily pushed aside these days. And there is no doubt the World Series Cricket movement was a turning point for our cricket.

I'm glad to say we've never looked back since those days.

Unfortunately, a lot of Australian cricketers don't appreciate just how much cricket means to the countries which make up the West Indies — particularly the poorer ones.

In this book Mike Coward and Michael Rayner have succeeded in looking at cricket as a part of everyday life in the West Indies. They take the reader on a journey beyond the cricket grounds. It is a book which captures the rhythm and excitement of life on and off the ground in our part of the world.

Vivian Richards
London
August 1991

CONTENTS

AUTHOR'S NOTE

The anthropology of cricket takes on another dimension in the West Indies where the game bonds people and places and gives the region a powerful international identity.
While it has become fashionable to condemn the elite West Indian cricketer for the manner in which he plays, Caribbean cricket offers more than is available elsewhere because it is an essential element of life throughout the archipelago. It is truly the game of the people and it is celebrated rather than merely played. This is particularly so in Trinidad which, on the evidence presented in 1991, may one day supplant Barbados as the hub of West Indian cricket.
In often up-tempo, down-beat societies cricket offers a precious opportunity for the young and ambitious and comfort to the old and weary. Everywhere it is played and watched by people of passion, energy and knowledge; people who prefer to smile.
After many years of waiting and wondering, it was a joy to be a part of such a ritual celebration of a great game.

PHOTOGRAPHER'S NOTE

Since my childhood when my father would regale me with stories of Captain Henry Morgan, the buccaneers, *El Drago* and the Spanish Main, and I would listen to Harry Belafonte croon songs like *Island in the Sun* and *Kingston Town* over the family's HMV radio, the Caribbean has always been intriguing and mysterious.
As a ten-year-old I became part of cricketing history by being among the ninety-thousand odd, record breaking crowd at the Melbourne Cricket Ground to see the West Indies battle against Australia. I vividly remember rolling off their elegant and stately names — Conrad, Seymour, Garfield, Rohan and Wesley.
In later years the mystery and intrigue of cricket and the Caribbean were heightened by fuzzy and vague images of flying bottles and burning grandstands. Somehow the childhood memories and those images just did not go hand-in-hand. Perhaps the time was right to clarify the situation and the seed for *Caribbean Odyssey* was sown.
I hope that I have been able to capture, through the lens, a sense of the colour, complexity, energy, hope and passion that I came to know as the West Indies.

ACKNOWLEDGEMENTS

We are very grateful that Viv Richards, one of cricket's most redoutable figures, happily consented to contribute a foreword. Ern Cosgrove worked with customary dedication to provide statistical tables and scoreboards and Ian Johnson willingly shared his recollections of Australia's first visit to the Caribbean. Thanks also go to Michael Bryant and Colin Balchin and staff at The Lab, Sydney for their professional processing of 400 rolls of film. We are also indebted to many people both within and outside the cricket community of the West Indies who so generously gave their time and their opinions. This is particularly so of Gus Logie and Tony Cozier.

Mike Coward and Michael Rayner
Sydney, August 1991

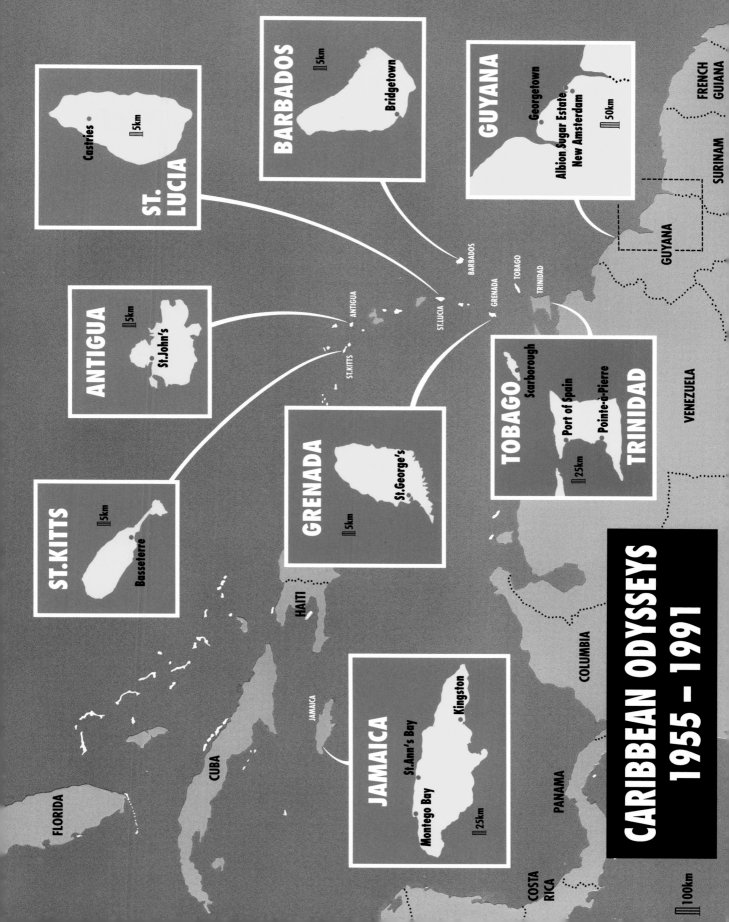

ST. LUCIA
Castries
5km

BARBADOS
5km
Bridgetown

GUYANA
Georgetown
Albion Sugar Estate
New Amsterdam
50km

ANTIGUA
5km
St.John's

ST.KITTS
5km
Basseterre

GRENADA
5km
St.George's

TOBAGO
Scarborough
Port of Spain
Pointe-a-Pierre
TRINIDAD
25km

JAMAICA
Kingston
St.Ann's Bay
Montego Bay
25km

FLORIDA
CUBA
HAITI
JAMAICA
ST.KITTS
ANTIGUA
ST.LUCIA
BARBADOS
GRENADA
TOBAGO
TRINIDAD
GUYANA
FRENCH GUIANA
SURINAM
VENEZUELA
COLUMBIA
PANAMA
COSTA RICA
100km

CARIBBEAN ODYSSEYS 1955 – 1991

CHAPTER ONE
A WORLD APART

"YOU SEE," CONFIDED THE ANTIGUAN businessman as BeeWee flight 418 made its final approach into St. John's, "cricket gives us the opportunity to compete with the First World. Actually we do it better and that is very important to us," he added with a beguiling smile.

He was light on his feet as he disappeared into the V. C. Bird International terminal and hurried past a large photograph of Isaac Vivian Alexander Richards which hangs from a central pillar in the lounge. That he did not pause to genuflect was mildly surprising given the tenor of the conversation throughout the short flight from Barbados.

Behind him were the elite cricketers of vastly different worlds. The West Indians, resplendent in maroon blazers and led by The Antiguan himself, had a spring in their step. The Australians, in green uniform and green with envy, were heavy in their tread as they filed through the building and into the canary yellow schoolbus belonging to the Ministry of Education: Government of Antigua and Barbuda.

The elite of Australian cricket took another tentative step into the Third World early in 1991 and in well practised fashion soon became disorientated and dispirited. As a consequence they were convincingly defeated by a tired and strangely fearful West Indian team generally thought to be withering on a vine

Previous pages: Ominous sign. Dark clouds shroud Sabina Park, Kingston as a solitary spectator contemplates what lies ahead. Above: Washing day at Bartica in the Guyana interior.

snaking from Jamaica, 772 km (479 miles) south of Florida in North America by way of Trinidad and Tobago, Guyana on the South American mainland via Barbados to Antigua 692 km (430 miles) north of Venezuela.

While publicists and propagandists the world over foreshadowed a shift in the balance of power by the end of the series for the Frank Worrell Trophy, history suggested the status quo would be maintained. And so it proved to be with the resourceful and resilient West Indies untroubled to complete their sixth consecutive successful defence of the trophy

barely six weeks after their first home defeat in a series of limited-over matches.

Australia's record in the Third World since the World Series Cricket apocalypse of the ancient game in 1977 exposes extreme deficiencies in the education, preparation and selection of international players. Furthermore, it adds substantial weight to the argument that the contemporary Australian cricketer is a force to be reckoned with only on his terms in his environment. Traditionally, a country's worth as a cricket nation has, to a large extent, been based on away performances in

"Australians all, let us rejoice ..." In Antigua, a smaller land girt by sea, Australian supporters at last had cause to raise the flag and sing the praises of their cricketers who won the final Test match by 157 runs.

vastly variable and challenging conditions. Indeed, it has been the ability of the West Indies to consistently win away from the Caribbean that has provided them with such an awesome reputation and the finances to maintain a modest but intensely competitive first-class domestic competition. Contemporary Australian cricket would be humiliated if judged by such criteria.

Since the Centenary Test Match at Melbourne in March 1977 Australia have won just ten of sixty-five off-shore Test matches and only three of thirty-four in the Third World — two in the West Indies, one each in the losing series of 1977–78 and 1990–91 and in Sri Lanka in 1982–83. They have tied one, against India at Madras in 1986–87, and lost fifteen and drawn fifteen. Before 1977 Australian teams won sixteen and lost just six of thirty-six Tests in the West Indies, India and Pakistan. So bleak is the record that the 4–0 victory in England in 1989 represented Australia's only success in any away series of three or more matches since 1975. While the regaining of the Ashes substantially lifted the morale of the Australian cricket community and justified an elaborate ticker tape reception through the streets of Sydney, it was patently clear twenty months later that too much importance had been placed in the achievement. It was too easily and quickly forgotten that English cricket was at its nadir in 1989 when despairing selectors summoned twenty-nine players in six Test matches.

AUSTRALIA'S TEST RECORD 1877-1991

Decade	*All Tests*					Decade	*Tests Outside Australia*				
	P	W	D	L	T		P	W	D	L	T
1877-80	4	2	—	2	—	1877-80	1	—	—	1	—
1881-90	28	8	4	16	—	1881-90	12	2	2	8	—
1891-1900	24	10	6	8	—	1891-1900	11	2	6	3	—
1901-10	34	17	8	9	—	1901-10	18	6	8	4	—
1911-20	16	7	3	6	—	1911-20	6	2	3	1	—
1921-30	33	16	10	7	—	1921-30	18	6	10	2	—
1931-40	33	19	5	9	—	1931-40	14	7	5	2	—
1941-50	23	18	5	—	—	1941-50	11	9	2	—	—
1951-60	57	27	17	12	1	1951-60	32	13	14	5	—
1961-70	68	21	29	18	—	1961-70	38	10	15	13	—
1971-80	87	34	26	27	—	1971-80	39	8	19	12	—
1981-90	93	26	36	30	1	1981-90	40	8	15	16	1
1991	8	2	4	2	—	1991	5	1	2	2	—
Totals	508	207	153	146	2	Totals	245	74	101	69	1

Note: Washed out Test matches 1890 (Manchester), 1938 (Manchester) and 1970-71 (Melbourne) have been excluded.

West Indian cricket may not have been at its zenith at the start of 1991, but it was still imposingly strong with its old warriors determined to make at least one more stand. Indeed, barely three months earlier they had kept the biting winds of change at bay by coming from behind to level a series in Pakistan which was promoted as the unofficial championship of the world by both the Urdu and English press. But for the brave and obstinate batting of Imran Khan and tyro Masood Anwar, the West Indies almost certainly would have achieved a famous victory in the final Test at Lahore. The quality of the tour performance coupled with the return to health of captain Vivian Richards gave the selectors Jackie Hendriks, David Holford and Irving Shillingford the confidence to ignore hysterical regional demands to overhaul a winning team for the visit by Australia. In the end they chose the same team for the five Tests, a feat accomplished previously only by England against Australia in 1884–85 and by South Africa when hosting England in 1905–06. Remarkably, the same XI also carried the standard in the last Test of the previous contest for the Frank Worrell Trophy at Adelaide Oval in February 1989.

At least in the minds of publicists bonded by a desire to reinvigorate Test cricket, the West Indies went from one "Clash of the Titans" to another. So rich and romantic is the history and lore of cricket between Australia and the West Indies that the international cricket community was full of anticipation as the psychological point-scoring began in advance of the eleventh contest for the Frank Worrell Trophy.

Forty-five years before they first played the West Indies in a Test match, Australia included a West Indian in their XI against England in the eighteenth Test match which was played at the Melbourne Cricket Ground in the first week of January 1885. Born at Hobart, the son of Barbadians lured to Australia by the prospect of gold, Sam Morris remains the only black man to have played Test cricket for Australia. During the West Indies first tour of Australia in the summer of 1930–31, the incomparable Learie Constantine met Morris. "At Melbourne we came across a West Indian, a coloured man who had played Test cricket nearly fifty years ago. It is an amazing story. He is a black Barbadian — it would be a Barbadian," recorded Constantine, a Trinidadian in awe of the extraordinary cricket heritage of Barbados.

That the West Indies toured Australia just two years after being accorded Test match status was, in part, due to the lobbying of Charlie Macartney, one of Australia's most distinguished cricketers. In 1928, two years after his retirement from Test cricket, the "Governor General" as he was so fondly known, had seen the West Indies in England and while they were trounced by an innings and some in each of the three Tests, he believed their cricket had a rare and exciting quality which deserved to be encouraged.

That quality was never more evident than in 1950 when having been beaten by 202 runs in the first Test at Old Trafford, Manchester, the West Indies won the next three matches by considerable margins to complete their first series win in England. The series which established the three Ws as maestri and saw Sonny Ramadhin and Alf Valentine spin their special magic captured the imagination of the cricket world and the following year led to the West Indies' first visit to Australia in twenty-one years. Australia won the series 4–1 and, while the visitors did not fulfil expectations, the contest was not as lopsided as the scoreline indicated and plans for a reciprocal visit were put in train. The administrations received encouragement and advice from the Australian Prime Minister, Sir Robert Menzies, a noted devotee of the game, and the Captain-General and Governor-in-Chief of Jamaica, Sir Hugh Foot, and in March 1955, three-and-a-half years before the death of Charlie Macartney in Sydney, Ian Johnson led the first Australian team to the West Indies.

In cricket and diplomatic terms the tour was an overwhelming success and not the abject failure so harshly predicted to Johnson by England captain Len Hutton during the Ashes tour of Australia which immediately preceded the exercise. Uneasy at the recollection of the bitter and controversial tour of the Caribbean by his England team early in 1954, Hutton made no attempt to mask his prejudice when talking to Johnson. "We were very much looking forward to the tour but a bit apprehensive after what the Englishmen said.

Hutton really went to town on them," Johnson recalled.

"As it happened it was a wonderful tour and there was no friction in the matches at all. We found people to be exceptionally friendly and we quickly re-established the good rapport we enjoyed in 1951–52." The relationship between the countries was further intensified in Australia in 1960–61 when Richie Benaud and Frank Worrell, the first black man to lead the West Indies outside the Caribbean, acted together to provide the kiss-of-life for Test cricket which was moribund at the close of the 1950s. In gratitude, cricket followers around the world lustily sang their praises. In Melbourne, a city passionate about its sport, half a million people lined the streets to bid a spontaneous and emotional farewell to the game's consummate entertainers. When the teams next met, in the Caribbean in 1964–65, they strove for the Frank Worrell Trophy. To the great shame of the West Indies Cricket Board of Control, the illustrious prize could not even be found for ceremonial occasions and for presentation to the victorious West Indies team in 1991.

Disappointingly, the Worrell Trophy lost some of its sanctity the first time it was contested and the only time it was on offer before Sir Frank Worrell's death from leukaemia at the age of forty-two in 1967. The visit of Bob Simpson's party in 1964–65 was clouded by controversy surrounding the bowling action of the redoubtable Barbadian Charlie Griffith. The Australians did not lodge an official complaint but their suspicions and grievances were aired by a number of journalists including Richie Benaud. The critics contended Griffith's terrifyingly fast yorker and bouncer were delivered with a different action and one which could not withstand scrutiny. But as was the case in England in 1963, the umpires found no fault with Griffith's bowling style and he played in all five Tests and took fifteen wickets at 32.00. A number of the Australian players took still and moving pictures of Griffith at the point of delivery and many local observers believed the preoccupation with a perceived injustice was a principal cause for their 2-1 series defeat. Writing in *Wisden Cricketers' Almanack,* the English journalist Alex Bannister said, in part: "The one cloud on the West Indies horizon, and which darkened the sunny relations between the two countries, was the argument caused by Griffith's action. At the end of the tour the simmering bitterness came to boil in articles published under (Norm) O'Neill's name. They, in turn, provoked an official protest from the Board of Control for cricket in the West Indies."

While the damage done was not irreparable the relationship between the countries lost its innocence. With the notable exception of 1972-73 when Ian Chappell's fledgling party recorded a celebrated 2-0 series success against an undirected opposition, subsequent visits by Australian teams to the Caribbean have been characterised by mistrust and uneasiness and punctuated with controversial incidents. Tensions

While basketball continues to gain in popularity cricket is still played on many a beach, savannah, roadside, carpark and building site throughout the Caribbean. Here young Jamaicans parade their skills.

increased markedly after 1975–76 when the crack Australian unit Greg Chappell inherited from his older brother, Ian, flogged the West Indies 5-1 before large and often aggressively parochial crowds in Australia. Clive Lloyd, who succeeded Rohan Kanhai as West Indies captain late in 1974, vowed never again to be humiliated in such a manner and pledged to construct a team of greater brilliance and ruthlessness to rule the cricket world. And while he succeeded beyond even his wildest dreams he never once forgot the disgrace of 1975–76. His successor, Viv Richards, also was badly scarred by the events of 1975–76 and fifteen years later he alluded to them on more than one occasion as he organised another successful defence of the Frank Worrell Trophy. The brothers Chappell, Dennis Lillee and Jeff Thomson, the principal engineers of the 1975–76 blitzkrieg, could not have imagined the profound effect their actions were to have on the way Test cricket was played throughout the world during the 1980s and into the 1990s.

To the West Indian, cricket is an essential and precious element of life, not an amusing, anachronistic pastime, and success and failure are seen in a context which extends well beyond the game's boundaries. In every victory and defeat there are racial, social, political, regional and economic implications. Although satellite television is hastening the Americanisation of the Caribbean and luring more children to basketball, cricket remains the pre-eminent sport and, with music and the rhythms of life, the passion of the people. Without cricket and, to a lesser extent, the University of the West Indies with its main campuses in Jamaica, Trinidad and Tobago and Barbados, there would be little other than a geographical denotation to identify the region. Since the disintegration of the infant West Indies Federation in 1962, cricket has provided a strong bond between the disparate countries which comprise the archipelago in the North Atlantic Ocean between North and South America and enclose the Caribbean Sea and the Gulf of Mexico. And while select politicians and economists endeavour to advance the cause of the emerging 13-State Caribbean Community (Caricom) and consider a common currency, cricket folk proudly point to the way the game has united so many of the territories.

"I would think that in our quest for regional integration cricket has been our saving grace," said Wes Hall, the Minister for Tourism and Sport in the Barbados government, a prince among yesterday's fast bowlers and a much-loved raconteur and humorist. "It has been the only thing that has pushed us forward as a people. There are five million people in the West Indies and another five million West Indians overseas. When we play a game those ten million people combine everywhere in the world to make us a very serious force. In cricket we are powerful but there's very little else that we can claim to be world champions in." In order to protect and parade the richness of the Caribbean cricket heritage, Hall

The Skyhawkers of St. Andrew's Church. A boy, a bat and a ball was once the ethos of Antigua. Since the advent of satellite television from the USA it is more like a boy, a basket and a ball.

yearns for the establishment of both a Hall of Fame and an Academy for the specialised and intensive coaching of the young.

Clive Lloyd, Test cricket's longest-serving captain, is among those who ascribe to the theory that the skipper of the West Indies cricket team is more powerful and influential than any political or social leader. In a sense, the fact that in 1988 Lloyd was asked to write the introduction to the voluminous history of West Indies cricket written by Jamaican Prime Minister Michael Manley serves to underscore his belief. In spite of indifferent health and pressing issues of government at a sensitive time in the history of Jamaica and the Caribbean community, Manley found

time to see some of the first and final Tests with the Australians in 1991.

The great responsibility of the office in such a complex and heterogeneous society was forcibly driven home to Viv Richards in 1990 when he ignored the history of cricket in the Caribbean and identified the West Indies team as an African team. His remarks provoked an angry response particularly in Guyana and cosmopolitan Trinidad and Tobago which have large and powerful communities of East Indian descent. Many people in the region believed his remarks confirmed the suspicion of an inverted racism within West Indies cricket. As politicians, religious leaders and the game's administrators howled in protest,

Richards moved quickly to defuse the situation when he said he "was dealing with a collective unit of people not just Africans. African Caribbean people include all the different nationalities of Caribbean people because of the struggles we have been through many a year ... I was speaking along those lines." In Trinidad and Tobago it was suggested by one politician that Richards should apologise before being allowed to enter the country.

In his conclusion to a memorable analysis of the situation, the insightful Trinidadian writer Ian McDonald, observed: "The statement undermines the foundation of a West Indian nation being painstakingly built on a non-racial basis. Cricket up to now is the great definer of our West Indian nationhood. I do not think I am exaggerating the importance of this issue. Cricket is that important to we West Indians. The captain of the West Indies cricket team is, in a very real sense, infinitely more important than any politician in the region. Tread carefully, therefore, Captain, lest you tread on our soul."

Vivian Richards is renowned for many things but not the lightness of his step in the middle or beyond the boundary. He is among the most stridently political of captains in the history of cricket and often to the consternation of the game's administration he has unapologetically used his office as a political platform. An awareness of, and a pride in Black consciousness has been the cornerstone of his doctrine as captain. He can be a confronting man whose attitude and actions serve to remind us that West Indies cricket is a product of slavery and colonialism and provides a vehicle for the fiercely proud West Indian to excel in the eyes of the world.

The West Indies is the only region where cricket is indisputably the game of the people and down the summers it has fired passions and ambitions and provided countless opportunities for young men to improve their lot in life. "But these days it is more than a way out: it's a very lucrative lifestyle," declared Wes Hall.

While cricket generally is seen as the one unifying force in the Caribbean and perhaps, in time, a

Winning smiles. Left: Ritual brushing as morning breaks at a shantytown in Port of Spain, Trinidad. Above: Michael Holding, who has made an impressive transition from fast bowling to fast analysing as a media commentator, at his busy service station in New Kingston, Jamaica.

21

catalyst for a renewed drive towards federalism, at the start of the 1990s the game was bereft of resources to withstand the extreme economic pressures of the times. At the time of the visit of the Australians the West Indies Cricket Board of Control was effectively bankrupt. But for the sponsorship of the international communication conglomerate, Cable and Wireless, and the Australian and European television rights negotiated by its marketing agents International Management Group (IMG), the WICBC may have found its bankers suddenly lacked benevolence. But at season's close not even such massive transfusions could avert a shortfall officially estimated at more than US$175 000. Costs for the Australian visit were more than US$2.5 million.

"We have an amazing amount of

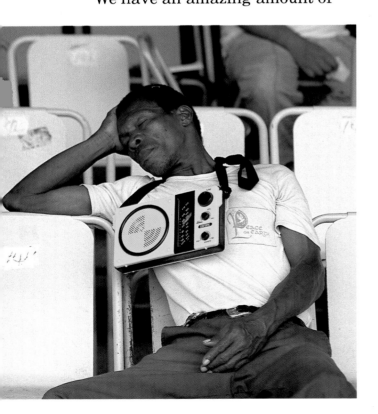

goodwill. I hope one day we don't run out of it," confided WICBC executive secretary Stephen Camacho in his unpretentious office in the 3Ws grandstand at Kensington Oval in Bridgetown, Barbados. Camacho, an affable Guyanese who, as an opening batsman, played much in the manner of an executive secretary in eleven Test matches between 1967 and 1979, has served at a difficult time in history, and in 1987 had to oversee the dramatic halving of the domestic competition as a cost-cutting measure. To his relief, the new sponsorship of the Jamaican company Denoes and Geddes enabled the unabridged competition to resume the following season and the six teams to compete for the Red Stripe Cup which is named after the company's internationally recognised brand of beer. So badly was the WICBC hurting that Camacho foreshadowed an end to five-Test campaigns which started in 1952–53 with the visit of Vijay Hazare's Indian team. By the mid-1990s he envisaged the West Indies hosting three-Test visits or playing five Test matches at three venues.

"The reality is we are dealing with small populations and depressed economies and small stadia. The fact of the matter is the majority of our costs are in hard currencies and with the devaluations in the various territories our real income is, in fact, going down and the real costs are going up," said Camacho. "The fees our players get are exceptional in terms of the per capita income in the countries they come from and are comparable to those paid anywhere

Above: House full. Spectators jockey for position on the steps of the Clive Lloyd grandstand for the limited-over international in Georgetown. Left: Off the air. Catnapping as more rain falls at Queen's Park Oval in Port of Spain.

in the world. In real terms we are trying to reward our players but we cannot earn money here in sufficient quantity and the board has done exceptionally well in getting appreciable guarantees for overseas tours. The money we get from overseas tours has merely gone to pay off the deficits of the home tours which means we have had less and less money to put into the development of our cricket. Unless we get money from some other place it is really the law of diminishing returns; real income is not appreciating and real expenses are."

The frequent devaluation of the currency in Guyana, Jamaica and Trinidad and Tobago has heightened the problems facing the WICBC whose executives increasingly find themselves drawn to the small Windward and Leeward Island groups and their stable East

23

Caribbean dollar. As early as 1960 Sir Frank Worrell predicted that by the end of the twentieth century the Lesser Antilles would play a major role in the future of West Indies cricket. "He was a prophet, really," said Wes Hall.

To Camacho's sorrow the future of Test cricket in his homeland Guyana with its borders to Venezuela, Brazil and Surinam becomes more clouded by the day. Until the late 1980s the land of the fabled El Dorado was an impressive earner for the WICBC but the heavy and repeated devaluation of the dollar has brought the co-operative republic to its knees. During the brief visit of the Australians the rate of exchange for the US dollar was increased from G$115 to G$127 and there was nothing but fool's gold for the board's coffers in Bridgetown. Yet while the country seemed at the point of disintegration the cricket community was generous in spirit, hospitable to a fault and took pride in playing the national anthem before the Test match, the only country to do so. But time passes slowly in Guyana, as the Australians discovered, and as evidenced by the letter to the editor of the *Guyana Chronicle* seeking a Hindu calendar for the Hindu year 2048 and an Arabian Islamic calendar for the Islamic year 1412.

Cricket may no longer be the exclusive pursuit of the young throughout the Caribbean but Test players have retained their exalted standing within society and are seen as appropriate role models for adolescents. In a valedictory interview in Guyana, Viv Richards exhorted adolescents not to use illegal drugs and to be restrained in their use of alcohol. In Port of Spain, his predecessor, Clive Lloyd, told business graduates that the "promise of progress in a nation lies in its youth". Furthermore, he said, the energy of a small band of West Indian cricketers had kept alive the promise of West Indian Federation and had clearly defined regional characteristics. Devout born-again Christian Ian Bishop, arguably the world's most exciting young fast bowler at the start of the 1990s, urged the youth of Trinidad and Tobago to act as responsible role models. Unable to play against Australia because of a serious back injury, the 23-year-old was speaking at a National Youth Rally, Exhibition and Presentation. "In winning a youth award one will find that not only have you achieved some form of excellence in your chosen field be it in community service, business, sport or education, but have created within yourselves a spirit of self reliance and also set yourselves on the road to a rewarding future," he told a rapt audience in Port of Spain.

At the same time there is a group of former players, Conrad Hunte, Wes Hall and Lance Gibbs among them, who believe that in the name of competitiveness and professionalism some of their successors have tarnished the good name of West Indies cricket. In April 1991, at the age of fifty-eight, Hunte returned to his native Barbados for the twenty-first anniversary of the Conrad Hunte Sports Club at Shorey Village in the north-east of the coral country. A distinguished batsman who averaged 45.06 with eight hundreds in forty-four Tests between 1957 and 1966, he has lived abroad since 1956 and among other business duties is honorary consul for Barbados in Atlanta, Georgia, in the USA. Known throughout the international cricket community for his involvement with Moral Rearmament, Hunte has vigorously advanced the cause of racial harmony and understanding and by his deeds endeavoured to achieve a regeneration of society by "complete honesty, purity and love" — the tenet of the movement. A magnificent orator, he first became involved with Moral Rearmament in Melbourne in 1960 when touring Australia under the inspirational leadership of Frank Worrell.

"At that time we were called to be, not just a sportsman in flannels, but a statesman for the West Indies," said Hunte. "It does sadden me that some of our top players are beginning to break the spirit of the game. It takes a strong mind and spirit to be able to absorb such high glory that sportsmen and film stars have. It is going to take strong leadership from the board, manager and captain to give us back not only the best cricket team in the world but the best sportsmen in the world. Some of us are very concerned about the image of West Indies cricket and we are working behind the scenes with some of our people to see if we can change that. There is no point in winning matches and losing the respect of the people."

As the 1980s gave way to the 1990s increasingly widespread anger and disappointment was expressed at the

High stakes. "Want some herb, man", someone called to Mike Whitney during the first Test match at Sabina Park, Kingston.

Memories. Conrad Hunte, businessman and honorary consul for Barbados in Atlanta, Georgia, sweeps away the cobwebs before wicketkeeper, Wesley Hall and slipper, Charlie Griffith. They were playing a special game to mark the 21st anniversary of the sports club which bears Hunte's name.

tactics employed by the West Indies to maintain their supremacy in world cricket. Unbeaten in a home Test series since 1972–73 and defeated away just twice in sixteen seasons after 1975–76 — by India in 1978–79 and New Zealand in 1979–80 — they were regularly and roundly accused of playing the game in a cynical and violent manner. While always blessed with extraordinarily gifted batsmen, fundamentally their success has been achieved by a seemingly endless line of fast bowlers often given to bowling consistently short while operating at barely twelve overs per hour. To many, the ruthless predictability of their cricket has become stupefying and time and again there have been loud and sustained appeals for the game's legislators to bring them to heel.

They are, of course, neither guiltless nor blameless but at the same time one suspects much of the bitterness and resentment has been born out of envy. For despite the game's modest and disjointed infrastructure in the Caribbean, the West Indies have been the consummate professionals of the modern era and have established the benchmark by which all cricket countries are judged. Immaculately groomed and highly self-disciplined they have established imposing standards in the execution of skills and in the scientific preparation of body and mind. Above all they have been consumed by a matchless urgency; a desire to better their lot in life.

The West Indies cricket team cannot be seen in isolation from the wider society of the Caribbean and therefore matters of colour and culture will not be pared away to make life more comfortable for the game's self-absorbed establishment in the First World. As black pride and black consciousness is a powerful and motivating influence throughout the Caribbean so it is within the elite cricket squad. While the first Test match was played in Melbourne in 1877 — forty-three years after the abolition of slavery in the Caribbean — it was to be another eighty-three years before Frank Worrell became the first black man to captain the West Indies outside the region.

"The West Indies cricket team has given West Indians a pride and a confidence in themselves," said Antiguan historian, teacher and journalist King Franki. "I think by and large the team has lifted black consciousness and Caribbean consciousness." King Franki, a Rastafarian who taught Viv Richards West Indian history at Antigua Grammar School, believes his former pupil has served the cause with distinction. "Viv is strident about black consciousness. He is with the people who want to stand up and regain some of the pride they have lost through all those years of slavery and degradation."

John Arlott, the distinguished English writer and doyen of the game's broadcasters, has always maintained that cricket mirrors perfectly the mood and attitude of Anglo-Saxon society. And there is irrefutable evidence that in the final years of the twentieth century, racism continues to torment societies the world over and make a mockery of

27

universal brotherhood and sisterhood.

Viv Richards has been deeply wounded by racist taunts directed at him throughout his career and his tolerance of his persecutors has diminished in mid-life. His supporters call him passionate; his critics say he is paranoid. Whichever, his pain is unmistakable.

"If you don't understand a people's culture you won't understand the people at all. Some people look at you and remember you as just being a slave. Some don't see the progress that has been made; that we have broken those particular chains. One is looking forward to us joining hands and living together but some people don't want it that way.

"On cricket circuits you will get 'black bastard' or 'jammy black' so and so. It's crazy. Some of them really look at you out there like you should be hunted. But I can tell you, no man is going to hunt me in this day and age. I take up the pursuing first. I'm prepared to die for that. These are my beliefs. No one is going to deny me the right to existence. I would prefer to die. These are the strong feelings I have and I will take with me. I have no fear in that particular way."

While the eleventh contest for the Frank Worrell Trophy was not completely free of racist innuendo, primarily it was distrust and disrespect which caused such bitter divisiveness among the players and their managers. On and off the ground tensions increased with each passing day and by the time the final Test was played in Antigua the teams were a world apart and Clyde Walcott, the president of the WICBC,

publicly lamented the fact that the series had been played in such a poor spirit. While Vivian Richards and Allan Border moved swiftly to allay fears of irreconcilable differences between such great adversaries, a number of their players could scarcely conceal their disappointment and disillusionment. They were irritated that the same core of players on each side had repeatedly caused disruptions and divisions without being brought to heel by captain, coach or manager. Unlike Allan Border, they did not believe the unpleasantness would be forgotten in future series.

Among those who felt ill at ease was Gus Logie who will forever remember the series for its association with the death of his mother, Augustina, the birth of his first child, Giovan, and the serious head injury he sustained in the first Test match. A courageous man and a devout Christian who carries the Bible wherever he travels, Logie bemoaned the sharp division of the dressingrooms. "The game has changed quite a lot. It is being fought more ferociously both on and off the ground. I think it could be enjoyed a lot more. It can be played hard but let's enjoy the camaraderie with the guys coming over and having a drink. But that's a bit difficult at this point of time. You don't know which way to turn. The people involved seem to be the most influential ones and people tend to take their lead from them. If they don't, it can be interpreted as a sign of weakness. I hope it doesn't reach the stage where you can't say 'Morning!' or 'Hi!' when you go out there. I would like to think that after cricket I can go to your country and enjoy something and you can come to mine."

When he was the last batsman dismissed in Antigua to give Australia just their second Test victory in eighteen years in the Caribbean, Logie, characteristically, picked his way through a swarm of excited supporters to congratulate Allan Border. It was a deliberate and powerful statement by Logie who despite the mixed emotions he experienced throughout the series, finished second to Richie Richardson in the batting averages.

Contact between the teams in Australia has been so concentrated since the World Series Cricket schism that grudges, prejudices and jealousies all too easily have been carried from one series to the next. The West Indies visited Australia six times between 1979–80 and 1988–89 for sixteen Test matches and myriad limited-over matches. Between 1930–31 and 1975–76 they toured on just five occasions and played twenty-six Test matches. Team management met at the start of the tour in Kingston, Jamaica, and talked politely of common objectives and *bonhomie* but it soon became evident that the get-together was a sham and the cultural divide could not be bridged. Trifling matters were allowed to fester, prejudices were paraded publicly, acidic kisses were blown and verbal exchanges and aggressive, intimidating posturings were as unseemly as they were commonplace.

As was the case on Bob Simpson's first visit in 1964–65 the international billing of the series as the unofficial championship of the world created further and unwanted pressures. The Australians, after so many abject failures against the West Indies throughout the 1980s, believed a historic victory was attainable. But they overestimated their achievement of winning the limited-over series and, for utterly inexplicable reasons, underestimated the power and capability of the West Indies fast bowlers. In the end they were crushed by a fading West Indian XI with an average age of 32.36 which was living in fear of failing in front of demonstrative crowds constantly demanding change. "I think this team has got one more big punch. I'm positive of that," Viv Richards told Australian journalists before the first Test match. Fear of failure is a powerful motivation in the West Indies where outstanding and

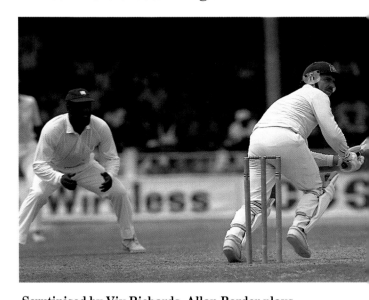

Scrutinised by Viv Richards, Allan Border plays neatly to leg in the final limited over match in Guyana. The skippers argued vehemently during the match.

consistent success is expected rather than merely hoped for. "When the West Indies team is doing badly it is amazing the way it affects the lives of the people because they identify so strongly," said Stephen Camacho. "We need to remain champions of the world. If you are champions you can negotiate. If you are ordinary, then people give you a game, sometimes," said Wes Hall.

Viv Richards is proud that ordinariness has been eliminated from West Indian cricket since the mid-1970s and is irritated that the establishment refuses to recognise the shift in power which has taken place within the game in that period. "Whenever the Ashes are being played one hears talk of 'proper cricket'. It's sad that someone can say that; dismissing the fact that we have competed against them. What were they doing with us? Mucking around or taking us for a ride? It is not very sensitive if you are dismissed that way. Statements like that will cause particular tensions."

It was, however, the less abstract and recurring issues of sledging, slow over-rates, intimidatory bowling and dishonourable behaviour which caused the greatest tension and led to such mistrust and malevolence. Although much of the professionalism of West Indian cricket was initially learned and honed in Australia at the time of the World Series Cricket movement, their players generally have always shunned sledging as an acceptable, defensible tactic. Sledging has become such a part of cricket in Australia that since 1981 it has been

defined in the Macquarie dictionary of Australian English as "the practice among bowlers and fielders of heaping abuse and ridicule on the batsman". It is a practice that has upset many West Indian cricketers, who, as a rule, seldom speak in the heat of battle. And those who do speak, notably Viv Richards and his deputy Desmond Haynes, assert they have modelled their technique on Australian cricketers.

"After being abused by a guy, you don't expect him to come over and say 'how are you going? You want a Tooheys?' You don't do things like that," said Viv Richards. "If I draw the sword, I draw the sword. When I draw it, that's it. It's the way we are brought up. You don't come and call me all sorts of things and then expect to come up and put your hand on my shoulder telling me that we are the best of friends. Forget about it."

Given the tensions which existed on the field and, by the final Test, in the boardroom as well, there was little fraternisation in the dressingroom as each team blamed the other for the acrimony. To some degree, the depressingly wet dry season which deprived the series of any rhythm obscured the extent of the conflict until the unholy and most public rows in the decisive fourth Test at Bridgetown, Barbados. On the first day at Kensington Oval Desmond Haynes, who was uncharacteristically terse and tetchy for most of the series, made a menacing gesture with his bat towards provocative Australian wicketkeeper Ian Healy. And on the final day, in the full flush of victory, Vivian Richards launched

The walk of a winner. Viv Richards strutting from Bourda, Georgetown after the
West Indies first victory at the ground for 26 years.

a personal attack of such vehemence against Australian coach Bob Simpson that it threatened the goodwill existing between the West Indies and Australian administrations.

Chewing on a fat, celebratory cigar while giving his post-match press conference in the bowels of the Sir Garfield Sobers pavilion, Richards gave vent to feelings uneasily harboured since he had first heard Simpson batting against Joel Garner and seen the nature of his appealing to umpire Ralph Gosein at Queen's Park Oval, Port of Spain, in March 1978. "He is a moaner and a bad loser. He's a very sour sort of a guy. I've seen him over a number of years and seen the way he operates. I may say that I'm not the greatest lover or

greatest admirer of Bobby Simpson. You treat people as you are treated," exploded Richards.

In the intervening years Richards accumulated considerable resentment towards Simpson and was irked by a recent reference to a perceived brittleness in the West Indies batting. For some time Simpson has been a vocal critic of many aspects of West Indies cricket and although he was not at the Bourda ground, Georgetown, when Dean Jones was controversially run out by Carl Hooper in the second Test, he questioned the morality of the dismissal. After Australia's only loss in a spectacularly successful limited-over series Simpson criticised the rules covering rain-affected matches claiming that a fairer system applied in Australia. "We don't feel it's a real loss," said Simpson according to a Caribbean News Agency (CANA) report.

The Australian party was astounded a Test captain could blatantly use a forum for team matters to state his personal views and demanded that Richards apologise. Given the importance of the series and the popularity of Barbados and Antigua as tourist resorts, the Australian Cricket Board (ACB) was well represented over the final two weeks of the tour and team manager, Lawrie Sawle, quickly mustered support for Simpson. Board chairman Colin Egar, Alan Crompton and Jack Edwards, delegates from New South Wales and Victoria respectively, Ian McDonald, the ACB media manager and Alan Davidson and Bob Radford, luminaries of the New South Wales Cricket

With a copy of *Wisden Cricketers' Almanack* in hand, Australian coach Bob Simpson heads for the umpires' room after the controversial dismissal of Dean Jones at Bourda.

Association, were on hand to add voice to the protest. But neither Richards nor the West Indies Cricket Board of Control were ruffled by the numbers and for some days there followed a Mexican stand-off punctuated by statements which brought no credit to either administration.

Each of Simpson's three visits to the Caribbean with Australian teams has been studded with controversy. His 1964-65 visit was overtaken by the furore surrounding the bowling action of Charlie Griffith and an umpiring controversy in Guyana which led to selector Gerry Gomez, a former all-rounder, being asked to make his first-class debut as an umpire in a Test match. To add to Simpson's pain Australia lost a series to the West Indies (2–1) for the first time. His next visit, in 1977–78, was more traumatic. Cajoled out of retirement to rally the establishment troops in the face of media tycoon Kerry Packer's marauders, at the age of forty-two he was in charge of a very modest team on a tour afflicted throughout by bitter incident and argument.

Confronted for two Test matches by the powerful West Indies World Series Cricket team, the cricket was overshadowed by an official objection to the amount of short-pitched bowling by Colin Croft; a crowd riot at Sabina Park which denied Australia probable victory in the final Test; and, a succession of umpiring controversies culminating with renowned Douglas Sang Hue no-balling off-spinner Bruce Yardley for throwing. And again, Australia were defeated, this time by the margin of 3–1. To what extent the memory of such misadventures affected his approach thirteen years later, particularly after being laid low with a viral infection and cellulitis in his right leg before the first Test, was a point of conjecture for critics throughout the tour. And that two of the critics were Ian and Greg

Chappell, with whom he has extreme ideological and philosophical differences, would have played on his mind. Writing for the Cable and Wireless official souvenir program, Ian Chappell declared: "The approach of Australian coach Bob Simpson will have a bearing on the team's performance. Simpson does have a tendency towards a siege

NAMING RITES

The kingly names of West Indian cricketers have long invited lyrical writing and commentary.

Since the West Indies entered the Test match arena at Lord's on 23 June 1928 scores of their cricketers have borne names which stir the emotion and evoke the wonders and mysteries of the polyglot lands of the Caribbean.

Invariably the names are elegant, and often they mirror the musical rhythms and vibrancy of the region. Sometimes they are amusingly esoteric, alliterative and splendidly excessive when judged by the standards of more conservative and unromantic societies.

Cricket is an integral part of life in the West Indies and it is not uncommon for parents to perpetuate the memory of a favoured cricketer when naming a son. In the opening game of the tour against a President's XI at Basseterre, St. Kitts, the Australians were confronted by the Antiguan fast-medium bowler Kenneth Charlie Griffith Benjamin. The closing match of the tour, the fifth Test in St. John's, Antigua, was officially scored by Benjamin's brother, Collin Everton De Courcey Benjamin. Another brother rejoices in the moniker of Rohan Basil Kanhai Benjamin. (Charles Christopher Griffith, Everton De Courcey Weekes and Rohan Babulal Kanhai are among the most celebrated of Test cricketers.)

Antiguan Test cricketers have had particularly grand names since Anderson Montgomery Everton Roberts paved the way for Isaac Vivian Alexander Richards and perhaps the most beautifully named of all the flannelled gods, Eldine Ashworth Elderfield Baptiste. They have been followed into the fray by Richard (Richie) Benjamin Richardson, Curtly Elconn Lynwall Ambrose, Winston Keithroy Matthew Benjamin and, in England in 1991, by Hamesh Aubrey Gervase Anthony.

Among many others Jamaica has given the cricket world Hophnie Horace Hines Johnson, Franz Copeland Murray (Gerry) Alexander, Maurice Linton Churchill Foster and Easton Dudley Ashton St. John McMorris, who was a broadcaster at Sabina Park during the visit by the Australians.

In Guyana, the birthplace of Berkeley Bertram McGarrell Gaskin, Sheik Faoud Ahamul Fasiel Bacchus and Colin Everton Hunte Croft, we met a Hindu devotee of the game called Compton Evans Balgobind (after legendary England cricketers and characters Denis Compton and Godfrey Evans) and worked alongside a capable young agency journalist called Urrell Bernard Wilkinson. It transpired that Urrell is the youngest of ten children and one of six to have been given the initials of his father, Ulric Bertram Wilkinson. With a measure of pride Urrell listed his siblings with barely a hesitation: Peter Ralston, Leslin Patricia, Relrick Bertram, Ulric Bellamy, Urneil Barrington, Maxine Wendella, Urles Beverley, Urland Bentley and Ulston Benton.

In essence, it is a matter of the game of the name.

mentality if things start to go wrong on tour, as he displayed in Pakistan on the 1988–89 visit, and if he inflicts this attitude on the team it will have an adverse effect on their great fighting spirit." In Antigua, Simpson was seen to remonstrate with Greg Chappell in front of the Viv Richards players' pavilion.

The uneasy meetings and terse statements also revived unpleasant memories for Colin Egar who managed Kim Hughes' team which performed so ingloriously in 1983–84 despite the superhuman achievements of Allan Border. Destined to succeed a frayed Hughes as captain ten months later, Border scored 521 runs at 74.42 — his epic unbeaten innings of 98 and 100 in the drawn second Test at Port of Spain immediately becoming part of the lore of Test cricket. The restless left-hander Wayne Phillips was the next most successful batsman with 258 runs at 25.80. It remains a blot on the Australian game that the tour is remembered as much for the indiscipline and poor sportsmanship of Hughes and some of his confreres as it is for Border's heroics. The Australians were defeated 3–0 and the West Indies did not lose a second innings wicket for the series.

That Richie Benaud, Ian Chappell and Greg Chappell were assigned by the Channel 9 television network to cover the series meant that the first and third Australian teams to the Caribbean also were represented throughout the series. Benaud, who played the first of his 63 Tests against the West Indies in Sydney in January 1952, was one of many in Ian

Johnson's party who enjoyed heady success in 1954-55. He took 18 wickets at 27.00 and from just six innings in five Tests scored 246 at 41.00 including the third fastest Test hundred in history (78 minutes) at Sabina Park, Kingston. Characteristically, Ian Chappell led from the front and headed the averages with 542 runs at 77.42 to engineer the success of 1972–73. His next visit in 1978–79 was made under the banner of World Series Cricket, the radical movement initially spurned in Australia but vigorously embraced by the West Indies unfettered by traditional ties and dreaming of a new professionalism and a new way of life. But the journey is remembered not for the revolutionary nature of the cricket but for the subversiveness of crowds at Supertests in Guyana, Barbados and Trinidad.

At Bourda in Georgetown, the Australian and West Indian players feared for their lives when they were trapped for two hours in their wooden dressingrooms as a crowd of 13 000 went on the rampage. In his book *The Wildest Tests,* the distinguished cricket writer Ray Robinson described the drama as "the most alarming ordeal endured by cricketers anywhere". The disturbances in Barbados were sparked by the reaction of West Indian opening batsmen Gordon Greenidge and Roy Fredericks to rulings by umpires Douglas Sang Hue and Ralph Gosein.

The calibre of umpiring in the Caribbean has long been a vexed and sensitive matter and, predictably, it was high on the agenda at the

Age is a state of mind. Excited Bajans show their solidarity for the ageing West Indian team after the 343-run victory at Kensington Oval.

debriefing. Overall, the standard was poor but while there were many misgivings about the competence of some officials, their impartiality was never questioned. The most damning indictment was that some umpires, notably Clyde Cumberbatch who incorrectly judged Dean Jones run out in the second Test at Guyana, appeared unfamiliar with the small print in the laws of the game and conditions of play for the Test and limited-over series. However, given its loud, if lone opposition to the concept of independent umpires, the Australian Cricket Board was not in

a position to offer any meaningful criticism. As has always been the case the umpires had to contend with extraneous pressures — particularly at Sabina Park where the pitch was inadequately covered — but none were caused by unruly spectators. The crowds, with a higher percentage of women than is the case elsewhere in the cricket world, were wonderfully exuberant, good-natured and exceptionally knowledgeable. And numbered among them were some of the game's most whimsical and endearing characters — King Dyal, Mac Fingall, Gravy, Mayfield and

Spirit of progress. Wherever he plays, Allan Border's ardent supporters are close at hand.

"Blue Food" Gabriel.

In the middle, however, there was no playfulness and humour. The unofficial championship of the world was both a struggle of attrition and the Mother of all Anticlimaxes. Viv Richards and Allan Border, however, were untroubled to justify the manner in which the series was played. In Antigua both made cathartic statements which reverberated around the cricket world and were greeted with incredulity by the establishment. "In my case it is a pleasure playing against the Australians because they are a tough sort of unit," said Richards. "We've got a couple of tough guys as well, and when you get two teams as tough as we are you are going to get a few little ill-moments here and there. We've seen that in this particular

series but I would like to believe that cricket will always be the survivor. There seems to be bad blood everywhere in cricket today. I think we need to respect this game of cricket and it is time for everyone to start realising that no one individual is bigger than this game of cricket."

Border, who like Richards conceded some of their minions had been shocked by the intensity of the conflict, defended the right of the modern professional to play Test cricket as ruthlessly as he saw fit. "Test cricket is not a waltz in the park any more like the good old days. It's a hard game and you are going to get clashes. When you are beating the hell out of an opponent you very rarely have any drama with him. But if he's sticking you as much as you are sticking him, that's when it gets a

Keeping up with the Joneses. Trendsetting Dean Jones intent on eliminating glaring errors in the field.

bit aggressive. When you see two sides really going at each other they have a hell of a lot of respect for each other." Their street-fighter views were not, however, shared by the majority of the protagonists.

Two of the greatest batsmen in the annals of the game, Richards and Border found it increasingly difficult to defy the passage of time and, as earnestly as they tried, neither could exert telling influence at the crease. Border, who in the final match equalled Sunil Gavaskar's record of 125 Test appearances, finished third in the averages with 275 runs at 34.38 but managed just one half century. Within three months of entering his 37th year, Border admitted he could be slipping as a batsman. Richards, teased mercilessly about what he terms his "no option hair cut", struck

two half centuries but returned only 174 runs at 24.86 to finish seventh in the averages. The week he entered his 40th year he suffered the indignity of having to dive to regain ground in a limited-over match at Port of Spain. And at Bridgetown he was put on his back and had his cap dislodged by a steepling delivery from Merv Hughes. Richards' protégé, Richie Richardson, topped the West Indies averages with 475 runs at 67.86 while Mark Waugh, Border's logical successor at number four, achieved the distinction for Australia with 367 runs at 61.17. Waugh also topped the bowling averages with eight wickets at 22.88 and took 10 catches, as many as wicketkeeper Ian Healy. And for good measure he played the most fantastic stroke of the campaign — a flat square cut for six against Malcolm

How sweet it is. Curtly Ambrose, the towering fast bowler from the village of
Sweets in Antigua, celebrates another success. He bowled with great intelligence
throughout the series for 18 wickets at 27.39.

Marshall in the decisive limited-over international at the Kensington Oval in Bridgetown.

Craig McDermott, who like Mark Waugh was only required for the last two Tests in the Ashes series which preceded the showdown, continued his stirring comeback by taking 24 wickets at 23.50. He was able to sweet-talk his garrulous mate Merv Hughes into sterling service (19 wickets at 31.00) but in unison with each member of the party bemoaned the fact that the lissom left-hander Bruce Reid lost his way as quickly as he had rediscovered it against England four months earlier. His demise along with the fall from grace of Terry Alderman, Michael Whitney, Stephen Waugh and Greg Matthews, who presented as an altogether different person and bowler in the West Indies, left Allan Border the quasi all-rounder, and Mark Waugh with too much responsibility as bowlers.

Conversely, Vivian Richards needed only to throw the ball to either Curtly Ambrose, Patrick Patterson, Malcolm Marshall and Courtney Walsh, a quartet Border believed to be as formidable as any fast-bowling combination of his time. Significantly, it was Marshall who produced the most impressive analysis (21 wickets at 20.18). As with 'keeper-batsman Jeff Dujon and Gordon Greenidge his place in the XI had been considered in jeopardy at the start of the series. Dujon, too, confounded his critics by completing a record-equalling 23 dismissals while Greenidge averted a mid-life crisis by amassing an unforgettable double

century just 10 days before his 40th birthday.

There was an unmistakable sadness in Clyde Walcott's voice when he breasted the microphone in front of the Vivian Richards players' pavilion at the Recreation Ground in St. John's and reproved the combatants for playing the Frank Worrell Trophy series in an unfriendly manner. Essentially, he charged them with violating the spirit of cricket between Australia and the West Indies.

Just 10 days earlier Walcott and Everton Weekes had made one of their periodical visits to the grave of their dear friend Frank Worrell at the University of the West Indies campus at Cave Hill in Bridgetown. As ever, on these occasions, they recalled their salad days and talked of the good times they'd spent together with Ian Johnson's first Australian tourists.

In those less hurried days before independence from Britain and the importing of the American dream and its candy culture and basketball there was a mateship between the cricketers of Australia and the West Indies which reached beyond barriers imposed by even the most bigoted of communities.

Only in Kingston where the cricket buff of 1954–55 was liable to ask for an explanation of the White Australia Policy before arguing the toss about the pace of Keith Miller and Ray Lindwall, was there painful evidence of a society in decay and visitors were cautioned to stay away from certain areas of the Jamaican capital. Thirty-six years later, Allan Border and his men were given a similar warning.

CHAPTER TWO
PRISONERS OF CIRCUMSTANCE

Jamaica and the First Test
Sabina Park ● 1–6 March 1991

THERE IS AN UNDERLYING AND INES-capable sense of menace in Kingston. And it is so pervasive that the visitor to the Jamaican capital feels conspicuous and unsafe outside the hotel compound and the rusted metal capsules which pass for taxis.

Joe Reid, a genial cabby given to handing out advice along with a winder for the windows of his ancient but indestructible Peugeot, was anxious to put minds at rest and authenticate the billboards which shout from the roadside: "Tourism is our business, let's protect it." With a casualness born of fifty years on the island Christopher Columbus called the "fairest isle eyes have seen", Joe disarmingly became a guide, indeed a guardian, given that we were prisoners of circumstance.

The dashboard of the taxi provided evidence of Joe's sensibilities and an insight into the philosophy of a poor and proud Jamaican. "Real men don't absue women", declared one sticker. "Keep your eyes on Jesus not the pleasures of this world" announced another. For good measure there was a drawing of a marijuana plant with the inscription: "Nature's way of saying, Hi!" Marijuana has long been a part of Jamaican culture and Joe's lean body rocked with laughter as he told of the two plants flourishing in the public gardens outside the city museum. A cardboard cutout of a United States $100 bill dangled tantalisingly from the rear-vision mirror. But outside the taxi the genuine article remained out of reach after the devaluation of the Jamaican dollar.

From the radio roared the upbeat rhythms belonging to the downbeat urban society. There was a time when Joe listened to the sound of FAME (Fraternity of Amazing Musical Expressions) but now the dial was set permanently on Irie FM, a reggae broadcaster which takes its name from the island jargon for excellent. And it was good to its name, providing a vehicle for the often hard-edged political and social observations of reggae guru Bob Marley, his son, Ziggy Marley, Jimmy Cliff, the Melody Makers, Bunny Wailer, Black Uhuru and Peter Tosh and their ilk. In Joe's mind reggae could easily withstand the concerted challenge from the mindless and

Above: "Tourism is our business": A sign of the times and a slogan to remind the locals and reassure the visitor to the troubled capital.
Left: A frenetic cyclist in Kingston.
Previous pages: Children living in uncertain times. Ricky Lugg and Roxanne Williamson at a fruit stall near Moneague outside Kingston.

43

Right of passage. Laden sugarcane trolleys, their pilots sweating and straining at the helm, are given right of way on market day.

chauvinistic DJ music. To him, reggae is an expression of his life, times and culture, and it gives him succour as the country he loves plunges deeper into darkness.

Community tension is inevitable as the 600 000 inhabitants of Kingston learn daily of corruption in the highest places, of economic regression and of the cheapness of human life in the ghettos. As Joe jockeyed for position in the traffic which regularly chokes the city, he tapped the steering wheel in time to a biting satire of Saddam Hussein and

George Bush. Alan Magnus, Keith Poppin and Jo Jo Stewart reached the conclusion that "We might as well get stoned and sing beer-drinking songs", a lyric and sentiment which seemed to encapsulate the mood of the city, if not the country.

We reached Sabina Park by way of the 19th century house which belonged to Bob Marley and now serves as an imposing monument to the reggae prophet. Sabina Park is dominated by the monolithic grandstand which serves as a shrine to George Headley. One of only four

Food for thought and fuel for work as a Kingston labourer seeks
sustenance in the heat of the day.

cricketers to have averaged more than 60 in his Test career, Headley occupies a place in the hearts and minds of Jamaicans akin to that reserved for Sir Donald Bradman by many Australians.

The upper tier of the Headley grandstand affords one of the finest views of Kingston. On the concourse at the rear of the incongruous corporate boxes, the neglected old city gives way to Kingston Harbour and the isthmus where the Norman Manley International Airport is situated. From the rarified atmosphere of the corporate cubbyholes one can see beyond the National Stadium and the track where Arthur Wint, Herb McKenley, Don Quarrie and Merlene Ottey signalled their prowess to the athletics world, to the Wareika Hills. It is here that bandits, drug traffickers and political activists take an oath of secrecy and hide from the law.

Farther away rise the striking Blue Mountains; nature's elaborate backcloth for cricket at Sabina Park. It is on the far side of the mountains

45

Sands of time. A workman ekes out a living dredging one of the rivers which wind through fern gullies in the beautiful heartland.

Ghetto maestro. Collie Smith (right) who climbed the wall taking tea with the great George Headley.

at 31.69) and the international cricket community mourned as his body was taken from hospital at Stoke-on-trent, Staffordshire to his beloved Jamaica where a crowd estimated at 60 000 attended the funeral.

Gerry Alexander, a fine cricketer and leader provided a precious insight into the exceptional stature of Smith when he said: "His passing is a tremendous loss to those of us who came to realise what a wonderful spirit of cricket he was." The cricket world was left to ponder the impact Smith would have made in cricket and in the wider community had his "wonderful spirit" been guided and nourished by Frank Worrell, the scholar and statesman who succeeded Alexander as West Indies captain for the watershed visit to Australia in 1960-61. The historic tied Test in Brisbane began fifteen months to the day after Smith's death.

In his eulogy, the governor of Jamaica, Sir Kenneth Blackburne, said: "The name of Collie Smith will long live as an example not only of a fine cricketer, but also of a great sportsman. He will provide inspiration for our youth in the future."

Today his "wonderful spirit" reaches out to the youth of the ghetto from a unique shrine in the covered quadrangle of Boys' Town School. Impressively and indelibly marked on a wall between classrooms is a chronological account of his life and times as a cricketer. With exuberant children aged from three to fifteen playing against or alongside the wall every day it is a powerful memorial which celebrates the vitality of life.

negativity as a worrying sign of mental weakness following the undisciplined cricket played in St. Kitts. In the absence of coach Bob Simpson, who was confined to quarters with a viral infection and severe cellulitis in his right leg, Border took it upon himself to remind his men of the extent of the challenge they faced.

The only member of the party to have played a full series in the Caribbean, he was anxious for each of his men to steel themselves for the task ahead; to develop the mental toughness to withstand the unique pressures of playing at Sabina Park. Since 1984 he had numbered the ground among the most difficult on which to play and, characteristically, he did not mince his words when openly addressing the fear factor.

"The crowds love it when we get bounced and if we get hit they like it even more. That is the way they are. And that takes a while to get used to, particularly in Jamaica where they are a bit parochial," he declared. "The rhythm and the noise of the crowd makes it a very different experience and it is difficult to maintain concentration."

By stumps on the second day of the scheduled four-day exchange with Jamaica, Craig McDermott and Mark Waugh had both been hit in the head by short-pitched deliveries from Courtney Walsh, and Border had vehemently rebuked a member of the crowd who had loudly rejoiced in their misfortune. Furthermore, each member of the Jamaican slips cordon had laughed derisively when Mark Waugh had made an ungainly attempt to avoid a steepling delivery and had been struck on the flap of the helmet which protects the temple. It was regrettable behaviour by the Jamaicans and Border smiled the smile of the pragmatic professional when it was suggested he had the gift of foreknowledge.

The power of Border's rhetoric became painfully clear and there was a foreboding atmosphere in the Australian dressingroom as one player after another examined the gaping wound above McDermott's right eye. "The ground battle has begun here, at least," said someone, alluding to events in the Gulf War. "The bastards, bastards," said another player as he watched Mark Waugh, head aching but unopened, return to the frontline. McDermott was bloodied but unbowed and made a point of getting to his feet as soon as the shock waves and nausea subsided. He paced the dressingroom

Born again paceman Craig McDermott's vision was temporarily impaired but he did not lose sight of his goals. Right: Courtney Walsh, who inflicted the damage, relaxing away from the maelstrom of the middle.

like a caged beast mouthing obscenities and swearing vengeance before being taken to hospital where the wound was closed with 10 stitches. He had, to use island vernacular, been well and truly licked.

"Excessive short-pitched bowling kills the game. And it could kill a player. He won't be the last bloke to be hit in this series," said Border with as much bravado as he could summon given that Bruce Reid, his principal strike bowler, had again succumbed to back pain and suddenly, cruelly, was at prohibitive odds to play in the first Test.

Border could scarcely conceal his surprise when Walsh, the Jamaican captain, received an official warning for bowling in an intimidatory manner. While he could not recall a precedent, he was unconvinced such a reprimand would herald a change in policy. Border simply reasoned that as members of the Jamaican police force, umpires Anthony Gaynor and Lindel Bell owed their continued existence to vigilance and courage.

Walsh was miffed at the intervention of the constabulary and bowled an off break in protest before withdrawing himself from the attack.

In mitigation he pointed to the uneven bounce of the pitch. Given he seemed intent on unsettling, if not upsetting, the Australians at the start of their three-month visit, his argument lacked conviction. Australia won the four-day match by an innings and 137 runs, despite the fact that ardent followers of Jamaica could not recall Walsh generating such threatening pace during the recent cheerless Red Stripe Cup campaign. At the same time Joe had much to do to convince the protagonists and observers that his Test match pitch would provide an appropriate platform for the first round of the world championship.

Intelligence gathered from diverse sources suggested to the Australians that the pitch would provide substantially more pace and bounce on the second day but it did not specify whether there was the likelihood of variable bounce from the start. As the elite cricketers of the West Indies regrouped for the first time since their outstanding tour of Pakistan, the Australians checked, double-checked and then re-checked their protective equipment. While anxious not to show their anxiety, they had been unsettled by a ball which had rocketed between the face grille and peak of McDermott's helmet. Dean Jones even considered reviewing his longtime decision to reject the grille because it restricted his vision. But in the end he repositioned his mouth guard, straightened his shoulders, defiantly held his head high and ventured into the midst of the most feared pack of pacemen in the world.

Although the regulations in place for the limited-over contests offered him a peace of mind and a sense of security unthinkable in a Test match, Jones's arrogantly combative batting provided a timely tonic for his subdued teammates.

When he first reached the Caribbean just short of his 23rd birthday in 1984 Jones had made only five appearances in one-day cricket and not bettered forty. In 105 matches in the intervening years he had established himself as a daring and innovative batsman, and, in the opinion of some judges, had earned the right to be ranked alongside Desmond Haynes as the world's finest player of the abbreviated game.

More than most of his contemporaries, Jones identifies with Welsh entertainer Shirley Bassey's memorable throwaway line: "Applause makes me drunk". Time and again he has been carried along on the tide of a baying mob, and the demanding and unforgiving crowd at Sabina Park challenged him to produce a vintage hand. Intoxicated by the occasion he offered them a faultless and undefeated 88 from 98 balls. Much to Border's relief Mark Waugh demonstrated his resilience and strength of character by supporting Jones with a delightful 67 from 61 deliveries. Since their success at the World Cup in India and Pakistan in 1987 the Australians have mastered the skills required to defend a total, and to muted applause from the capacity crowd of 15 000, achieved victory by 35 runs.

For the ambitious Australians the limited-over competition was an incidental consideration from the outset. Nevertheless, psychologically they were immeasurably stronger after inflicting the first home defeat on the West Indies in five years. Given they had eliminated the swaggering Jamaican team three days earlier, their high spirits and sense of optimism were justifiable. But their excitement was tempered by the news that Bruce Reid was sore and despondent after bowling an uneventful seven overs and would be overlooked for the Test match.

Charles Morris Joseph rose before the

Craig McDermott swore vengeance after being cut above the right eye against
Jamaica. He was good to his word, returning the match figures of 8-128
in the first Test. Here he appeals against Gordon Greenidge whom he dismissed in
both innings.

Bruised, bloodied but unbowed. Gus Logie, tape covering seven stitches beneath his right eye, extricated the West Indies from the mire with a bold, undefeated 77.

eighth wicket fell at 166 in the 55th over, he played with his customary chirpiness and in the end was unconquered on 77 with 12 boundaries. With Dujon (59) he added 68 in 88 minutes for the ninth wicket and cajoled Patrick Patterson into such service that a further 30 runs were added for the last wicket. He left the ground to a standing ovation and returned to the team's hotel for rest. During the night he was told that his mother, Augustina, had died.

In just 23 overs a rejuvenated and singleminded McDermott had formally announced to the West Indian cricket community the intentions of the Australians. He had bowled with intelligence and genuine pace and had no qualms about pitching menacingly short. His rich reward was five wickets in an innings for the third time in as many Tests since his recall against England two months earlier. That he had outwitted Viv Richards the very moment the modern master was celebrating his 8000th run in Test matches gave him particular pleasure.

Preceding the tour Allan Border had spoken regularly of the need for reliable and uplifting opening partnerships if Australia was to prosper against the game's most accomplished fast bowlers. While he never lost faith in the rich abilities of Geoff Marsh and Mark Taylor, their repeated failures against England had caused him anxiety. After their partnership of 157 which gave Australia a 10-wicket success at the start of the Ashes campaign in Brisbane they had averaged just 20.75 in the next four Tests.

From the moment they arrived at St. Kitts, Marsh, Taylor and David Boon deliberately spent more time together, and as often as was sensible, reminded each other of the need to constantly watch the ball from the hand of the bowler. "Watch the ball" became a creed to be intoned with religious fervour every day. To Border's satisfaction their conscientiousness was rewarded when it mattered most.

Proud, strong and uncomplaining, Marsh and Taylor played with courage and exemplary self-discipline. They wore their determination to succeed and at the end of every over as they doffed their helmets to drain the perspiration, exhorted each other to maintain concentration and observe the creed. To the thinly disguised annoyance of the pacemen they offered a stroke only when it was required, and then only one within the realm of their capabilities. They would not be hurried or intimidated and barely flinched when struck on an unprotected area of their bodies. Even when he needed to replace the helmet grille after a mishap against Malcolm Marshall, Taylor remained calm and focused. By the 37th over his confidence and judgement was such that he counterpunched with a pull against Courtney Walsh. To that point neither Taylor nor Marsh had contemplated executing the pull or hook. Their partnership of 139 in 3 hours and 18 minutes was only the fourth century opening stand against the West Indies in ten years and the first since Graham Gooch and Chris Broad had displayed comparable resourcefulness for England at Nottingham in 1988.

In the proud name of the brotherhood, Boon built significantly upon the foundation, and, despite the irksome losses of Border and Dean Jones (who had another aberration against an off-spinner), had reached 71 without blemish or bruise by stumps.

While they were irritated beyond measure at the West Indies coldly calculated slow over rates, the Australians argued at strategy meetings that the tactic need not necessarily count against them. In some circumstances, they reasoned, it would be possible to score freely in the last session when Richards was surrounded by jaded fast bowlers and needing to lift the tempo in order to meet the daily quota of 90 overs. As though to prove the point Boon ensured 121 was added in a 43-over, three-hour, final session and although the crowd grew restless the Australians scored an imposing 4–292 from 90.3 overs for the day. It was a humbling day for the nervously uncertain West Indians and a revelation to peripheral internationals 12th man Brian Lara, Phil Simmons, Jimmy Adams and Cleveland Davidson who had been pressed into service in the field.

The folly of underestimating the mental toughness and resourcefulness of the hard-nosed West Indian professional was graphically demonstrated on the third day. Despite Mark Waugh's extreme discomfort against the steepling delivery the Australians reached 4–329 and salivated at the prospect of a lead in the region of 180. But in the face of an extraordinary assault from Patrick Patterson they lost their last six wickets for 42 runs and in the end were grateful for an advantage of 107. To the unrestrained delight of his hysterical Jamaican compatriots Patterson struck McDermott a bruising blow on the shoulder as he powered his way to an impressive 5–83 from 24 overs, the last four wickets coming at a cost of three runs from 19 deliveries.

The crowd in the Headley grandstand rose as one as Patterson and the defiant Boon left the ground. It was problematical how much of the applause was directed at Boon who after 5 hours and 43 minutes had become the eleventh Australian to score ten centuries in Test matches. He had seemed indestructible throughout the epic innings and had barely winced when hit flush on the chin by a bouncer from Patterson. He had even made time to counsel and comfort Mark Waugh who psychologically, at the very least, had paid dearly for his failure to watch the ball from the hand.

With the daring and arrogance which has long characterised West Indian batting Haynes and Greenidge, an incomparable opening combination, erased the deficit of 107 in just 124 minutes from 29.1 overs. So frenzied was Haynes's scoring as he moved beyond 6000 runs in Test matches that by stumps the West Indies had achieved an overall lead of 80 and with eight wickets held a marginal advantage. But had Richie Richardson not survived an emphatic appeal against Mark Waugh at 2–178 the Australians could have claimed

Solemnly intoning the creed of the upper-order coterie, David Boon batted for
6 hours and 25 minutes for a valiant undefeated century. Here he plays through
the legs of Gus Logie.

So near, yet ... Adventurous part-time bowler Mark Waugh draws an error in judgement from
aggressive century-maker Richie Richardson.

the ascendency. Such was the evenness of the contest.

Sunday worshippers filed into churches and into the tents of the travelling charismatic ministries dotted about the inner suburbs as the protagonists wearily left Sabina Park, giving thanks for the approaching rest day. On the radio a preacher exhorted his listeners to reject the ganja culture and put their shoulders to the wheel. "Work is not a sin. Work is not a mistake," he declared.

The Jamaican work ethic and the work practices of the groundstaff at Sabina Park became major topics for community discussion after it was discovered water had seriously damaged the pitch and surrounds. The players were prepared for some delay given the ferocity of the rain late on the rest day but none had expected the scene of devastation which greeted them when they arrived at the ground and gingerly made their way to the middle. To their dismay the bowler's approach at the northern end was a bog and serious leakages along the seams of the covers had left several damp spots on the pitch. Furthermore, there was a wet and potentially dangerous indentation just short of a length at the northern end. It appeared as though an unsuspecting groundsman had rocked backwards on his heels before the covers had been removed. The tension was palpable as umpires David Archer and Steve Bucknor made their first inspection and players gathered in small groups speaking softly, confidentially. It was patently clear there would be no play

on the fourth day and the gates to the grounds were kept firmly shut.

Joe was close to tears as he endeavoured to supervise the cleanup and restoration work. While he maintained a diplomatic silence it seemed he had been stripped of some of his authority and he gestured contemptuously towards a man spraying organic fertiliser on the worst affected areas. He also argued with members of the Kingston Cricket Club who loudly demanded an explanation for such a state of affairs. The previous year rain on the rest day had caused the fourth day of the first Wisden Trophy Test to be abandoned with England tantalisingly close to their first victory in thirty matches with the West Indies since 1974. Much to the relief of Graham Gooch, and, one sensed, the Jamaican Cricket Board of Control (JCBC), England enjoyed their fleeting moment of glory in the last over before lunch on the fifth day.

Rex Fennell, the president of the JCBC and his predecessor, Allan Rae, were conspicuous by their absence as present and past players and commentators roundly accused the authorities of incompetence and obstinate neglect of responsibility. That Joe and his two full-time assistants and twelve casual labourers were compelled to work with such primitive equipment was the most damning indictment of the hierarchy.

It was common knowledge among the groundsmen that two new and sponsored covers were frayed when delivered to the ground and had been

Hellfire. In his desperation to redress the damage caused by the hopelessly inadequate covering of the square, crestfallen curator Joe opted to burn raked sawdust on the muddy pitch. Australian observers were aghast.

taken away and glued. Other covers were stretched at the seams and holed, and the drain pipes used to anchor rather than drain the synthetic covers were badly rusted. Ironically, the oldest and biggest of the nine covers was the most functional but for reasons never satisfactorily explained it was positioned not on the square but over the unuseable practice pitches on the eastern side of the ground.

So severe was the damage to the bowler's approach that Joe initially was uncertain as to the appropriate course of action. After the ineffectual burning of some of the sawdust raked across the mire he decided on an extensive reconstruction of the worst affected area. With a thick wooden board he hollowed out the mud and replaced it with new soil ferried by wheelbarrow from the lee of the Headley grandstand. For binding he scattered grass clippings through the layers of soil and then used a light hand roller and the heavy electric roller to compact the morass. But it remained a shifting surface and 51 minutes before the scheduled tea adjournment umpires Archer and Bucknor abandoned play for the day.

The intensely proud Jamaican sporting community was outraged at their loss of face throughout the cricket world, and editorial writers who had been preoccupied with heady matters of capital punishment and government scandal joined their colleagues on the sports pages in a sweeping condemnation of the country's cricket authorities.

67

Emotions ran so high that Clive Lloyd reiterated his call to the International Cricket Council to set up a crisis fund for Third World cricket countries, while noted critic Tony Cozier was harangued by a group of disenchanted Sabina Park groundsmen. Seven members of the casual groundstaff confronted Cozier in the telex room of the media centre and said they were affronted by remarks he had broadcast about their work practices. They were appeased, however, when the phlegmatic Cozier said he had broadcast an appeal for them to be issued with rain coats and boots.

There was further tension on the final day when, to the relief of highly agitated spectators, beleaguered umpires Archer and Bucknor ruled that play would resume after lunch. Initially, neither Richards nor Border was satisfied conditions were safe. "In the process of finding out if it is dangerous, do you want someone to die out here? I don't want to come out and find the ball whizzing round my nose," said Richards tersely. As it happened only one delivery behaved abnormally and Richards, on the eve of his 39th birthday, surpassed Sir

FIRST TEST

at Sabina Park, Kingston 1, 2, 3, 5, 6 March — West Indies won toss

WEST INDIES

		Min	Balls	4s			Min	Balls	4s
G. Greenidge	c & b McDermott	27	134	80	3	c Healy b McDermott	35	136	89	5*
D. Haynes	b McDermott	8	33	21	—	c Healy b McDermott	84	169	128	14
R. Richardson	c Healy b Hughes	15	36	27	3	not out	104	318	233	15
C. Hooper	c Marsh b Hughes	0	10	6	—	b McDermott	31	102	80	3
V. Richards	c Hughes b McDermott	11	25	21	2	not out	52	183	147	5*
G. Logie	not out	77	167	110	12					
J. Dujon	c Marsh b Hughes	59	210	166	7					
M. Marshall	lbw b McDermott	0	1	1	—					
C. Ambrose	c & b Waugh	33	72	47	6					
C. Walsh	lbw b McDermott	10	26	14	—					
P. Patterson	b Hughes	4	33	20	—					
Sundries	(6LB, 13NB, 1W)	20				Sundries (15B, 6LB, 6NB, 1W) 28				
Total		264				Three wickets for 334				

Fall: 33 (Richardson), 37 (Hooper), 57 (Richards), 68 (Greenidge), 75 (Haynes), 75 (Marshall), 144 (Ambrose), 166 (Walsh), 234 (Dujon), 264 (Patterson).

Fall: 118 (Greenidge), 134 (Haynes), 216 (Hooper).

	O	M	R	W		O	M	R	W
McDermott	23	3	80	5		24	10	48	3
Whitney	21	4	58	—		17	3	55	—
Hughes	21.3	4	67	4		22	5	79	—
Matthews	11	2	28	—		25	2	90	—
Waugh	6	1	25	1		13	6	20	—
Border						10	3	21	—

Batting Time: 379 Min. Overs: 82.3

Batting Time: 455 Min. Overs: 111

* denotes six (Richards 2, Greenidge 1)

Garfield Sobers as the West Indies highest run scorer in Test matches. Border, who on the second day had become just the second man to score 9000 runs in Test cricket, was among the first to offer his congratulations. The match will be remembered for individual accomplishments.

Rain clouds encircled the grounds as Gus Logie and David Boon were feted for their bravery and brilliance and Rex Fennell formally apologised for the fiasco. But so inadequate was the ground's public address system that his regrets were unintelligible to the faithful in the grounds who deserved so much more. Later they were told he had said: "The facts about what happened have been fully reported and we take the blame for it. It spoiled a wonderful game which was heading for a great finish and we apologise to our guests and friends from Australia."

As they left to resume their lives, heavy rain fell on Charles Morris Joseph's beloved and uncovered square, black goats nuzzled debris piled at the bottom of the embankments and someone, with a commendable sense of timing, lit a joint.

AUSTRALIA

			Min	Balls	4s
G. Marsh	c Dujon b Ambrose	69	198	117	10
M. Taylor	c Hooper b Patterson	58	237	151	3
D. Boon	not out	109	385	243	9
A. Border	c Dujon b Ambrose	31	98	72	4
D. Jones	c & b Hooper	0	3	3	—
M. Waugh	lbw b Marshall	39	144	107	3
G. Matthews	c Dujon b Patterson	10	57	27	1
I. Healy	lbw b Walsh	0	5	4	—
C. McDermott	b Patterson	1	17	15	—
M. Hughes	c Hooper b Patterson	0	1	1	—
M. Whitney	b Patterson	2	13	8	—
Sundries	(4B, 23LB, 21NB, 4W)	52			
Total		371			

Fall: 139 (Marsh), 159 (Taylor), 227 (Border), 228 (Jones), 329 (Waugh), 357 (Matthews), 358 (Healy), 365 (McDermott), 365 (Hughes), 371 (Whitney).

	O	M	R	W
Ambrose	30	3	94	2
Patterson	24	1	83	5
Marshall	22	3	57	1
Walsh	23	4	73	1
Hooper	21	7	37	1

Batting Time: 582 Min. Overs: 120

Match Drawn

Men of the Match: D. Boon & G. Logie. Umpires: D. Archer & S. Bucknor.

12th Men: B. Reid (Aust.), B. Lara (W. Ind.). Rain washed out play — 5 March

CHAPTER THREE

PRAISE THE GODS

Guyana and the Second Test
Bourda ● 23–28 March 1991

WITH THE STRENGTH OF A SOUL chosen by his God to rail against man's inhumanity to man the Dean of St. George's Anglican Cathedral prayed earnestly for the welfare of the Test cricketers of Australia and the West Indies.

STAYING ON

"To you, comrade Lloyd, welcome."

Taking his cue from the beaming female principal, Clive Hubert Lloyd stood tall before the students of Queenstown Community High School in Georgetown.

For a moment or two he was silent, lost in the mists of time. Only yesterday, it seemed, he had sat in this very room and dreamed of tomorrow. But it had been in another age, when his alma mater was called Fountain A.M.E. (African Methodist Episcopal), when his country had a compelling vision of independence from Britain, and the Caribbean community demanded the West Indies cricket team be captained by a black. It was a period of reform and of hope. But within five years of independence in 1966 the country had begun to lose its way and its brightest and most celebrated people.

Now, at a time of utter hopelessness throughout the sparsely populated land of unrevealed beauty, Lloyd addressed the school assembly as an expatriate Guyanese, a resident of England and a citizen of the world. In recognition of his exceptional deeds as a cricketer and leader he had been awarded an honorary Master of Arts from Manchester University, created an honorary officer of the Order of Australia and twice decorated by the government of Guyana. Raised in an unpretentious home around the corner from the school, Lloyd had become one of the world's most accomplished and thrilling batsmen and fieldsmen and carefully constructed and nurtured the most powerful cricket team of the modern era.

At the age of forty-six and broader in beam and girth, he was a celebrated visitor to his homeland and the gathering listened quietly, appreciatively to his reminiscences and to his carefully chosen words of encouragement.

At much the same time the hierarchy of Guyanese cricket met again and resolved to offer Lloyd the position of national coach. As with every stratum of society the cricket community had been seriously affected by the country's decay and officials yearned for a return to the days of the early 1970s and 1980s when first-class and limited-over trophies were proudly held aloft. But along with the academics, doctors, lawyers, teachers and priests, cricketers had joined the exodus of notable citizens. Of the country's most eminent former players only Roy Fredericks and Basil Butcher remained. Lloyd, his cousin Lance Gibbs, Alvin Kallicharran, Rohan Kanhai, Joe Solomon, Steve Camacho, Colin Croft and Faoud Bacchus had all sought greener fields and observed from afar the exploits of the country's contemporary internationals, Roger Harper, Carl Hooper and Clyde Butts.

While Butcher had repaired to Linden in the south of the country, Fredericks, as the adviser on sports to the Prime Minister, Comrade Hamilton Green, had ensured that the influential cricket fraternity was represented in government.

One of Guyana's most distinguished sons, for twenty years from 1963 Fredericks had proudly borne his country's standard on the cricket fields of the world and played in fifty-nine Test matches as a daring left-handed opening batsman, occasional slow bowler and exceptional close fieldsman. In 1982-83 he had been feted again by the people when at the age of forty he briefly put aside his responsibilities as a junior minister in government, adopted a role of player–manager and joined forces with Lloyd to transform the

Clive Lloyd, a son of Guyana, a resident of England and a citizen of the world, holds court at his alma mater in Georgetown.

Guyana team. After seven desperately poor seasons Guyana became the first country to win the first-class and limited-over titles in the same season and in his only Shield innings Fredericks, the great patriot, scored 103 against Trinidad and Tobago and 217 against Jamaica.

"It was my choice to remain in Guyana. It had nothing to do with politics. It was an emotional factor," he said. "I wanted to come back. I didn't want to live outside. I played my cricket outside but when I finished I wanted to come home and stay here. Men have to live their own lives and if they feel they can bring their family up in a better standard of living then that is their choice."

The Minister for Sport in 1981, when the government served a deportation order on England cricketer Robin Jackman because of his ties with South Africa, Fredericks had graduated from a tough school and ten years later was mentally prepared for the seemingly unavoidable backroom fight to retain Test cricket in Guyana.

The repeated devaluation of the country's currency had led to increased speculation that by 1993 the financially embarrassed West Indies Cricket Board of Control would have no option but to remove Bourda from Test match intineraries.

"This community needs cricket more than any other community in the Caribbean. But clearly we are under pressure. We might not get another Test match," he admitted heavily, clearly discouraged at the small crowds which attended the Test match with Australia for which he was the adjudicator. "I would have thought the match would have brought out the people but the budget had just gone through and the dollar was devalued about 40 per cent. I suspect that caused the problem as it is expensive to travel and the price to go to the game is very high."

Significantly, given the complex racial and social mores of the region, he admitted to a concern that the absence of cricketers of East Indian stock in the West Indies team would contribute to the Co-operative Republic of Guyana growing further apart from the rest of the Caribbean cricket cartel.

He confided he would help himself by plying his trade at the cricket. He too, was in no doubt that the rains would stay away; that the Dean's prayers would be heard.

Given the paralysis of the economy it was problematical how many people could afford to reach the Bourda ground. The increase in petrol prices was such that the expense of private and public transport was as daunting as the cost of admission. The hardest hit were the Berbicians from New Amsterdam, 80 km (50 miles) south-east of Georgetown as the macaw flies. Renowned as much for their knowledge of cricket as for the prized fruit and vegetables they sell at the bustling and colourful Bourda market, the annual Test match pilgrimage of the Berbicians is a part of the lore of West Indies cricket. Since 1954 when Barbadian Clyde Walcott moved to Guyana as inter-colonial captain and zealously took the game into the hinterland, Berbicians had set out one or two days in advance of a Test match, crossed the Berbice River and, by any means possible, made their way to Bourda. There they set up camp and by the flickering light of a kerosene lamp or wood fire drank, gambled and spoke passionately of the deeds of clansmen Rohan Kanhai, Alvin Kallicharran, Basil Butcher, Roy Fredericks and Joe Solomon. It is said that on occasions revellers slept through a day's play. Now all but the wealthy few would be dependent on the radio broadcast and on the coverage of the *Berbice Weekly*, a tabloid which is published monthly by Andrew Carmichael, its ambitious

22-year-old proprietor, editor and principal writer.

By international standards admission charges were inexpensive but to the impoverished and disillusioned Guyanese they were prohibitive. A series package to the limited-over international and the Test match cost either G$2000 (A$21.24) or G$1500 (A$15.91) — the equivalent of five or six weeks salary for many workers. A daily ticket in the grandstand cost G$200 (A$2.12) while admission to the rails, as the outer at Bourda is called, was pegged

Above: A woman of bearing and good humour in Bartica. Right: The universal language of cricket. Children in a polyglot society find common ground at Bourda.

at G$100 (A$1.06) and, to the basic schoolboys stand in the south-eastern corner of the ground, at G$50 (A$0.53). Outside the ground, men who could remember Learie Constantine, George Headley, Patsy Hendren, Les Ames and Wally Hammond strutting their stuff at the ground were reduced to begging for a ticket. "It's a bad time, boy. It's a bad time, boy," said one man despairingly.

"People are under tension here and for many it is a matter of trying to exist, not to live," said Dean Goodrich, a citizen of both Guyana and England. "Basically this is a religious country although not everyone necessarily runs off to church, mosque or temple. But there are few atheists and many people are returning to the church because, I think, they have lost faith in human powers."

Dean Goodrich bemoaned the passing of the egalitarian society of the mid-1970s when the rich revealed a social conscience and the streets were safe for the visitor to walk at night. A year earlier, when the England cricket team was in Georgetown, Dean Goodrich was accosted at night by one of the city's infamous "choke and rob" hoodlums and knocked to the pavement. The authorities were convinced his assailant mistook the Dean for a tourist. At an informal signing of the cathedral visitors' book Dean Goodrich was able to empathise with Greg Matthews who had a gold chain and wedding ring torn from around his neck in a lightning daylight robbery in the city. But through the

Given the economic climate, the "Freedom stands" were a popular choice at Bourda.
Patrons were at risk when Viv Richards faced Greg Matthews.

good offices of the police with an entree to "Big Daddy" and his nefarious colleagues in the underworld the jewellery was returned to Matthews and an amnesty declared for the duration of the Australians' visit.

Yet for all the official and unsolicited warnings about the omnipresent dangers of Georgetown the capital was in a welcoming and festive mood. The City Fathers even ensured the street lights were illuminated throughout the night. Nevertheless, at G$120 (A$1.30) per city drop it was prudent to take a taxi for even the shortest of journeys after dark.

Those among the touring party who felt confronted by the realities of Georgetown were able to remain in the Pegasus Hotel across the way from the United States embassy — an edifice rivalling the Russian legation for obscene ostentatiousness. While they felt confined to quarters the players suffered few privations in their Atlantic Ocean seawall enclave which offered a daily cricket rate of G$17 500 (A$185.69) for a twin room — approximately the annual income of a worker on the revised minimum wage. It was here, adjacent to one of the two swimming pools in the city, that the players basked in the glory of their triumph in the limited-over

The spectacular wooden architecture of the capital is reflected in the impressive gabled pavilion of the Georgetown Cricket Club.

series and dreamt of a fourth one-day victory and a comparable conquest in the Test match.

When battle for the one-day series was resumed before the only full house of their visit to Guyana, the Australians received unexpected and vociferous backing from the majority of East Indian supporters who did little to disguise their contempt for Viv Richards. Indeed, an Australian XI had not received such heartfelt support outside Australia since Allan Border's 1986 visitors to Hindu India played a limited-over international in the politically sensitive Muslim state of Kashmir.

Those of East Indian extraction substantially outnumbered those of African blood and the divisions and tensions within the crowd mirrored the separateness of the communities in the towns and villages. As the Australians reaffirmed their superiority at the compressed game, the crowd grew increasingly restless and abusive and loudly demanded changes to the team. Richards, who does not enjoy playing in Guyana, stopped proceedings when Courtney Walsh was hit on the hand by an unidentified object thrown from within the Lance Gibbs stand. Richards sauntered to the boundary to report his concern to the Guyanese cricket authorities and to oversee the medical treatment for Walsh who, just three months earlier, had been struck by fruit hurled by an agitated spectator in the dying stages of a tense Test match in Lahore, Pakistan. As the Guyanese police searched for the offender, a bottle was thrown in the direction of Desmond Haynes from the packed south-eastern stand at the other end of the ground. An experienced campaigner who had been entrusted with the captaincy in Pakistan, Haynes quickly and quietly put the bottle out of harm's way.

The behaviour of the crowd surprised the Australians and prompted a strong editorial from an indignant sports desk at the *Guyana Chronicle*.

"We have always respected the maturity of the Guyanese cricket supporters who flock the Bourda ground whenever an international tour comes around," proclaimed the newspaper. "But to say the least we were appalled at these incidents. We do not dispute the right of the individual to support whatever side he wants. But that support should not degenerate into 'boos and jeers'. And what was even more repulsive was the senseless throwing of bottles at our own West Indian players. The Caribbean has a proud cricketing record for decades now and we would not want that image to be tarnished by a misguided few — and certainly not in this dear land of ours."

The atmosphere was unpleasant and in time the tension spilled on to the field of play. Vice-captain Desmond Haynes shouted at a provocative Mark Waugh after being

controversially adjudged leg before wicket to Peter Taylor, and Allan Border lost concentration and was dismissed for sixty after an on-going argument with the testy Richards. Border infuriated Richards by exercising his right to seize on a ball which slipped from the hand of gentle medium-pacer Phil Simmons. Border ran to meet the delivery which sat up mid-pitch and with a good deal of ceremony smashed it over mid-wicket

for six. Richards left Border in no
doubt that he disapproved of his
action and their shouting match
intensified during a drinks interval.
To the first ball after the break Border
was caught at the wicket driving
extravagantly at Courtney Walsh.

While such high drama was played
out around him Geoff Marsh
maintained his concentration and
steely resolve to ensure Australia's
fourth success in twenty-three days.

Compelled to chase for the first time
in the series, Marsh judged to a
nicety the tempo of the innings and
was undefeated on 106 when the six-
wicket victory was achieved with
nine deliveries in hand. It was his
second consecutive and ninth limited-
over century and it took his aggregate
of runs in the series to a startling 349

Above: A place in the rails at Bourda cost G$100 per day, a third of the minimum weekly wage. Left: The formidable spectacle of Curtly Ambrose at the point of delivery. He returned the match figures of 4-109 from 55.4 overs.

at 87.25. As was the case in Barbados in the decisive fourth match, his most telling support came from Border. They added 124 in 97 minutes in an enterprising third wicket partnership — the perfect complement to their critical stand of 146 in 95 minutes at the Kensington Oval a week earlier. They had reason to be grateful to Craig McDermott and Merv Hughes who each completed remarkable second spells as the West Indies lost their last six wickets for 34 runs in the last 10 overs. It was an astonishing capitulation after Richie Richardson, with his second 90 of the series, had played so intelligently to build on the splendid foundation laid by Desmond Haynes (58) and Phil Simmons (34). McDermott finished with 3–29 to boost his aggregate of wickets for the series to 13 at 12.75,

while Hughes, preferred to Bruce Reid, took 3–23.

As the ecstatic Australians toasted their success with the carbon-purified, sterile-filtered Tropical Mist pure artesian well-water bottled by an enterprising local brewery, there began yet another inquisition into the state of West Indian cricket. On this occasion attention was focused on the unprofessional conduct of the fast bowlers who between them had dispatched 14 no-balls and 11 wides. Furthermore, 10 no-balls were scored from, bringing to 35 the number of bonus deliveries presented to the Australians. Eight bowlers offended during the five-match series, including off-spinner Carl Hooper and medium-pacer Phil Simmons who between them conceded 35 no-balls and 34 wides. Curtly Ambrose (16),

Tony Gray (16) and Courtney Walsh (13) were the other main culprits. Everyone, it seemed, had an opinion on what was widely interpreted as the regression of a once mighty West Indies team.

In the service sheet for St. George's Cathedral on Palm Sunday Dean Goodrich formally welcomed, on behalf of the diocese, the West Indian and Australian teams and all other visitors to Guyana. Unable to resist the urge to editorialise, he added: "The one-day international was an enjoyable game, but the West Indian bowling showed indiscipline in the superfluity of wides and no-balls." In the next paragraph the Dean reminded his parishioners of the need to bring a candle for the Vigil and First Mass of Easter.

By the time the Christian community celebrated Palm Sunday and the Hindus the sacred occasion of Ramnowmie, the birth anniversary of Lord Rama, the pride of West Indies cricket had regained poise and much of their credibility over the first two days of the Test match. Despite the continued absence of Bruce Reid, the Australians entered the fray with a justifiable optimism. But it proved to be seriously and sadly misplaced. If they believed they had gained a precious psychological advantage with their outstanding performances in the one-day series it was not evident in the manner they approached the Test match. From the moment Border won the toss to gain first use of a pitch brimful of runs they were consumed by an unexplainable defensiveness and uncertainty. The self-confidence and assertiveness so keenly displayed in the one-day series vanished in the face of relentless and highly intelligent fast bowling. Sensing the Australians' uneasiness, the West Indies pacemen immediately slowed the over-rate to ensure they controlled the tempo from the outset. To the chagrin of the Australians, the West Indies bowled 11.85 overs per hour and had the light not failed, play on the first day would have continued to 7.07 pm local time — 92 minutes after the scheduled close.

In Kingston, upper-order stability and enterprising batting by David Boon enabled the Australians to counter the tardy over-rate by scoring 121 in a 3-hour, 43-over final session. But at Bourda the new ball fell due in the seventh hour and with ruthless efficiency, Curtly Ambrose and indefatigable Malcolm Marshall removed both the belligerent but befuddled Dean Jones (34 in 170 minutes), and Greg Matthews, in successive overs to leave Australia a nervous, unconvincing 6–249 from 83 overs. But for the resourcefulness of Mark Waugh and Ian Healy who added 101 for the seventh wicket, the sterling work undertaken by Geoff Marsh (94 in 5 hours and 25 minutes) would have been utterly wasted. Waugh, seemingly unscarred by his harrowing experiences at Sabina Park, played with such poise for his 71 that Clive Lloyd publicly declared him the most accomplished legside player in Test cricket. It was a remarkable tribute given that the nonchalant Waugh was appearing in only his fourth Test match. But there

The last line of resistance is broken. For the second time in the match Allan Border
falls victim to wily Malcolm Marshall.

was no other comfort for the Australians who toiled painfully for 9 hours and 48 minutes for 348. Smarting from the counterpunches so boldly thrown at them in Jamaica, the West Indian fast bowlers had swiftly and ruthlessly reasserted their superiority. Bowling at the leisurely tempo of an over every 5.02 minutes they exploited the slowness and uneven bounce of the pitch by varying their pace while maintaining unerring accuracy.

Contentiously slow over-rates and breathlessly fast scoring rates have been the most striking characteristics of contemporary West Indian cricket. And when they occur in conjunction an irresistible force is created and unleashed on the hapless opponent. At team meetings the Australians

pledged stoicism and a preparedness to ride out any tempest. But not even a familiarity born of constant contests since the great schism of the late 1970s could prepare them for the savagery of the attack by Richie Richardson and Desmond Haynes.

With Viv Richards and Gordon Greenidge showing signs of mid-life uneasiness, Richardson and Haynes reached Bourda as the West Indies principal and most feted batsmen. Moreover, each boasted an exceptional record against Australia — Richardson having scored 1210 runs at 52.60 with six centuries in 16 Tests and Haynes 1790 runs at 45.89 with four hundreds and 12 half-centuries in 24 matches. And while little importance could be attached to the second innings in Jamaica, both

The scoreboard tells the sorry tale. Plucky Ian Healy watches Patrick Patterson administer the last rites as Australia nears a Test defeat for only the second time in 24 months.

had quickly re-established their authority over the Australian attack — Richardson with an undefeated 104 and Haynes, who had averaged a startling 109.00 for Barbados in Red Stripe competition, a whirlwind 84.

Furthermore, had the Australians analysed Richardson's record at Bourda they would have understood the urgent need to batten down the hatches. He went to the middle boasting an average of 91.5 having scored 185 against New Zealand in April 1985 and 194 against India in March 1989. By early afternoon on the third day he had increased to 731 his aggregate of runs at an average of 104.4.

Of average height but deceptively strong in the upper body, Richardson played with awesome power and

ruthlessly, methodically dismembered the Australian attack. As his game is based as much on instinct and reflex as on formal and sound technique, he can be susceptible at the start of an innings. On this occasion, however, he was in imperious mood from the outset and his consistent square driving against the fast bowlers was of rare quality. Indeed, the eminent commentator Tony Cozier was moved to compare his square driving with the very best offered by Everton Weekes who was renowned for his execution of perhaps the most thrilling and sensual of all strokes. He required just 60 balls for his 50 and 116 for his 100. Yet still he was not satisfied and for good measure revealed a greater surety in his judgement and footwork against slow

The pervasiveness of American pop culture. Forlorn and bankrupt Georgetown is no barrier to Ninja Turtle merchandisers and marketers.

Richie Richardson imperiously driving Greg Matthews for six during his
unforgettable innings of 182. David Boon's discomfort is understandable.

bowling as he reached his 150 from just 198 deliveries.

Much to his despair, Allan Border was unable to stem the flow of runs, let alone believe with any conviction that any of his bowlers had the capability to break the dazzlingly brilliant stand. In the end, and primarily at the insistence of Dean Jones, he reintroduced himself to the attack in the 69th over. He has such little regard for his ability as an orthodox left arm spinner, he invariably has to be cajoled into service. In his third over (and eighth for the innings) he elicited an error of judgement from Haynes (111) and so ended the extraordinary partnership of 297 in just 305 minutes and 70 overs. Border was relieved rather than excited at his success, subdued in the knowledge that he had no option but to assume the role of principal slow bowler and that Viv Richards and Gus Logie, among others, remained in the wings.

Haynes and Richardson had the immense satisfaction of spectacularly changing the course of the match and adding substantially to their second wicket record against Australia. At Adelaide in 1988–89 they had contributed a comparatively modest 167. Seemingly distracted by Haynes' dismissal, Richardson contributed just 19 more runs before he was trapped leg before wicket by the indomitable Craig McDermott for 182.

When Richardson had reached his century, the more ardent and excitable of his many Guyanese supporters had run past unconcerned policemen to embrace him, to hoist him high to receive the acclamation of the crowd and to present him with money. Indeed, there was a momentary hiatus to proceedings while he transferred to his pockets notes of substantial denominations which had been stuffed inside his shirt and the waistband of his flannels. In the privacy of the dressingroom he realised he had been given more than G$1500 (A$15.90). "They are in love with me and that's their way of expressing their appreciation."

For 5 hours and 44 minutes (and 242 deliveries) he had held spellbound the small crowds, and he left to a standing ovation flushed in the knowledge that he had scored his fourth century in five Test matches against Australia and at the age of 29 had surpassed Clive Lloyd and Larry Gomes as the West Indies' highest century scorer against Australia. "The Australians talk a lot and are very aggressive and that seems to motivate me," Richardson told journalists and commentators bewitched by his record of a century every 3.8 innings against Australia. "When you have people at you all the time you can't let up. You want to concentrate all the time."

Such imperious batting brought the Australian bowlers to their knees; the stoicism promised at team meetings forgotten by all but McDermott in the pain and sweat of endless pursuits into the deep. With Michael Whitney, Merv Hughes and Greg Matthews beaten into submission, Border's worst fears were realised as first Carl Hooper, and then Viv Richards and Gus Logie, turned the screws. Ahead of his doting home fans Hooper

Excited fans ran to embrace Richie Richardson when he reached his thrilling
century from just 116 deliveries. They showed their appreciation by plying
him with money.

Leading from the front. The inability of the specialist bowlers to stem the flow
of runs compelled Allan Border to assume the role of principal slow bowler.

caressed his way to 62 while Richards blasted 50 and Logie crafted 54. Richards, despite the discomfort of a stomach disorder, savaged the crestfallen Matthews, striking him for three sixes in five balls. Two off-drives cleared the Rohan Kanhai grandstand and threatened the welfare of those perched precariously in the freedom stands, the saman trees outside the ground. To complete Matthews' humiliation, the balls were retrieved from alongside the filthy canals on the far side of Regent Street at the southern end of the ground. Partially restricted by the dislocated little finger of his right hand and seemingly bereft of defensive bowling skills, Matthews was in his 100th over since his previous Test wicket — England captain Graham Gooch at Sydney eleven weeks earlier — when he unexpectedly dismissed Hooper.

Consequently, as the West Indies total increased in multiples of four and six — 318 runs came in blows to, or beyond, the boundary — Border had no choice but to assume the guise of premier slow bowler. Rotating his left arm and making light of the stiffness brought about by such a rare sortie into the attack, he bowled with admirable control and even extracted some slow turn from the placid pitch. To his undisguised surprise he also took wickets and so revived memories of his remarkable match analysis of 11–96 in more conducive conditions in Sydney in January 1989. Even given the West Indies' well-documented weakness to the ball turning to the off, Border's achievement in taking four wickets in nine deliveries without conceding a run was extraordinary.

Indeed, he was embarrassed. "I was really annoyed I didn't bowl more. To think I had 5–51 when they were 9–532. That's ridiculous."

For the first time in 122 Test matches he was required to bowl 30 overs in an innings and at the age of thirty-five suddenly was confronted with the possibility of playing the balance of the series as a quasi all-rounder. Not even a final analysis of 5–68 could ease his disappointment at Australia's numbing deficit of 221. Despite losing their last five wickets for 40 in 19 overs, the West Indies amassed the imposing total of 569 in 10 hours and 54 minutes — their highest Test score for seven years and only four runs short of their best return against Australia in the Caribbean at Bridgetown, Barbados, in 1964–65.

From the moment Richardson picked up the trusty but fractured cudgel he had loaned to a friend to play club cricket in Antigua the previous weekend, there was an inevitability about the defeat of the Australians. In the end they were overwhelmed by 10 wickets with the furore surrounding the dismissal of Dean Jones deflecting attention from another consummate performance by the fast bowlers, again splendidly led by Ambrose who was rewarded with his 100th wicket in his 25th Test.

But in the victors' dressingroom there was no overt sign of remorse over the run-out of Jones. There was, however, a powerful, pervading feeling of relief at such an emphatic victory after a dismal limited-over campaign. That they were the first West Indian team to win at Bourda

JONAH JONES

The wounding dismissal of Dean Jones roused the international cricket community from its reverie and provoked animated debate about the ethics and etiquette of contemporary cricket.

Howls of indignation reverberated around the cricket world following the instinctual running out of Jones by Carl Hooper after he had been bowled by a no-ball by Courtney Walsh. Yet at Bourda, where the deed was done as Australia strove to avert an innings defeat on the fourth day, there was reasoned reaction despite the growing uneasiness between the teams.

The pragmatic professionals and purists were polarised, as commentators, editorial writers, politicians and even the Roman Catholic Archbishop of Trinidad, Anthony Pantin, made sweeping and sometimes self-righteous judgements.

Of the key figures in the high drama only umpire Clyde Cumberbatch was in an indefensible position. Unlike captains Allan Border and Viv Richards he could not plead ignorance in mitigation. Had he not made such an astonishing error in cricket law the incident would not have occurred. Under two laws Jones should not have been given out and the integrity of Richards and Hooper would not have been publicly challenged.

Jones, perturbed by a sudden loss of form after a productive and thrilling limited-over series, had faced six balls in 10 minutes when he was bowled by Walsh for three. A frenetic soul, in one abrupt movement he left his crease, tucked the bat under his arm and, crestfallen, headed for the pavilion. He had not heard Clyde Duncan's call of "no-ball" nor seen the umpire's arm held wide to signal the illegal delivery. By the time he had responded to Border's anguished cries to regain his ground Carl Hooper had emerged with the ball from the gully region, ceremoniously uprooted the stump and led a robust appeal. At square leg, Cumberbatch, standing in his eleventh Test in as many seasons, either was unaware of the relevant laws

or suffered a blackout for he unhesitatingly agreed to the demand. Duncan, whose first verdict in Test cricket five days earlier had been palpably wrong, made no move to intercede.

Law 38 (2) states: "If a no-ball has been called, the striker shall not be given out unless he attempts to run." At no stage did Jones attempt to run. He was also entitled to the protection of law 27 (5): "The umpires shall intervene if satisfied that a batsman, not having been given out, has left his wicket under a misapprehension that he has been dismissed."

As the West Indies players huddled together and tried to reach consensus on the legitimacy of the decision, Border turned away from the retreating figure of Jones and swore vehemently. His hissing and cussing was born of frustration and not of perceived injustice and he made no move to speak with Jones, Richards or Cumberbatch. It was not until he reached the pavilion for the tea adjournment and examined the laws of the game in a *Wisden Cricketers' Almanack* hurriedly borrowed from the press enclosure, that Border realised Cumberbatch had made a grave error. With cap and *Wisden* in hand, Australian team-manager Lawrie Sawle approached the acutely embarrassed officials, but in their hearts the Australians realised the decision could not be rescinded.

Australian coach Bob Simpson did not see the incident but was swift in his condemnation of the West Indies for engineering the dismissal. "It's a little sad that should happen; that the fielding team should even do it," he told Australian journalists after returning from a practice session with the other members of the touring party. Simpson was, however, presupposing that Richards knew the laws and was prepared to recall Jones.

Throughout the ground and beyond, opinions were sharply divided and Border, annoyed at not knowing the laws, did not share Simpson's view. "There is no animosity on our behalf, whatsoever," he told a press conference. "We probably would have done the same thing. I don't have

Oblivious to umpire Clyde Duncan's call of "no-ball" and to Allan Border's anguished cries,
Dean Jones heads for the pavilion after being bowled by an illegal delivery.

problems with it. If it happens again, I will. We accept it as one of those freak things that happen. It was such a horrendous set of circumstances. So stupid."

Not everyone was so gracious and Richards, who is generally unappreciated in Guyana, was the butt of some stinging and incessant criticism by those who believed Jones should have been recalled. But Richards, intent on engineering a victory which might silence the team's burgeoning number of strident critics, had no feelings of guilt. And no blame could be attached to Hooper, anxious to atone for missing straightforward gully and slip catches in Australia's first innings. A gifted but surprisingly diffident player, he had trusted his instincts and reflexes to effect the dismissal in front of his adoring home crowd.

Jones, a garrulous and incorrigible soul, bore no grudge towards Hooper and did not expect Richards to call him back. When asked whether he would have recalled a batsman in similar circumstances Jones smiled sheepishly and said he made it a rule not to answer hypothetical questions. That such misfortune should befall Jones, who is numbered among the more competitive of Test cricketers, was an irony which did not escape the attention of his teammates.

A week earlier in the final match of the limited-over series he had been run out for eleven when he had wandered from his crease after surviving a leg before wicket appeal against Tony Gray. A tall, lean athlete, Gray casually retrieved the ball and in one smooth action threw down the wicket. On this occasion, Cumberbatch correctly judged Jones to be short of his ground.

Not even Border's immediate forgiveness won a reprieve for Cumberbatch and he was not asked to stand again in the series. At the end of what some pundits believed would be the last Test match at Bourda, an effigy of Cumberbatch was dangled from a noose and made to dance a macabre farewell to the Australians.

since Garry Sobers engineered a 212-run victory against Bob Simpson's Australians in 1964–65 provided further cause for celebration and Viv Richards drank champagne when he spoke effusively of his pride and unshakeable faith in his men. The success was the appropriate response to those who had dared to question the greatness of the team, he declared. "To the next critic I will say: 'Were you in Guyana? Did you see that?' What took place there was the perfect answer to those shouting certain things; the various corners calling to axe this and axe that!"

At the other end of the pavilion

with its high wooden walls covered with fading photographs of those who served when the territory was at first Demerara and then British Guiana, Allan Border could but lament the continued absence of Bruce Reid and ponder what might have been. A week earlier, after the heady success of the one-day competition, he was convinced a watershed victory was within Australia's grasp. In his heart he thought sufficient momentum had been established. Instead, there was the emptiness of defeat for only the second time in twenty-two Tests since January 1989. The realisation that no

SECOND TEST

at Bourda, Georgetown 23, 24, 25, 27, 28 March — Australia won toss

AUSTRALIA

			Min	Balls	4s		Min	Balls	4s
M. Taylor	lbw b Patterson	0	10	7	—	lbw b Ambrose	15	45	52	1
G. Marsh	c Hooper b Patterson	94	325	201	12	b Walsh	22	61	125	3
D. Boon	c Dujon b Marshall	7	56	31	1	c Dujon b Marshall	2	17	24	—
A. Border	b Marshall	47	148	88	4	c Dujon b Marshall	34	131	209	3
D. Jones	b Marshall	34	170	93	4	run out	3	7	10	—
M. Waugh	c Dujon b Patterson	71	232	135	7	c Richards b Ambrose	31	75	92	4
G. Matthews	c Dujon b Ambrose	1	6	4	—	c Dujon b Marshall	16	46	65	1
I. Healy	run out	53	176	102	4	run out	47	151	120	4
C. McDermott	lbw b Patterson	1	10	7	—	c Dujon b Patterson	4	41	22	—
M. Hughes	b Ambrose	0	17	10	—	c Patterson b Walsh	21	65	115	4
M. Whitney	not out	1	12	6	—	not out	0	14	12	—
Sundries						Sundries			
(6B, 8LB, 23NB, 2W)		39				(17B, 6LB, 28NB, 2W) 53			
Total		348				Total 248			

Fall: 3 (Taylor), 24 (Boon), 124 (Border), 188 (Marsh), 237 (Jones), 238 (Matthews), 329 (Waugh), 346 (McDermott), 346 (Healy), 348 (Hughes).

Fall: 32 (Taylor), 43 (Boon), 67 (Marsh), 73 (Jones), 130 (Waugh), 161 (Border), 172 (Matthews), 187 (McDermott), 241 (Healy), 248 (Hughes).

	O	M	R	W		O	M	R	W
Ambrose	31.4	9	64	2		24	5	45	2
Patterson	24	1	80	4		14	5	46	1
Walsh	24	2	81	—		23	4	55	2
Marshall	23	3	67	3		15	2	31	3
Hooper	13	3	37	—		18	6	35	—
Richards	1	—	5	—		4	2	13	—

Batting Time: 588 Min. Overs: 116.4

Batting Time: 457 Min. Overs: 98

season. According to the folklore of Trinidad and Tobago the flowering of the magnificent poui heralds the rainy season.

The welcoming and vibrant twin-island republic of T&T, as it is fondly known, was grey, wet and subdued for each of the three visits by the Australians between 7 March and 11 April.

The rain came with such frequency and intensity that it damaged much more than the short-term ambitions of the cricketers and their masters. At the height of the April deluge, the ceiling of the Parliament Chamber in the great Red House caved in forcing a postponement to sittings of the Senate and the House of Representatives. There were mud slides in the lush Maraval Hills, roads and footpaths subsided and frogs emerged from swollen drains. "Has dry season sprung a leak?" asked the front page of the tabloid, *Daily Express*. The sober, even solemn, broadsheet, *Trinidad Guardian*, pursued a more scientific path and quoted a meteorologist's belief that the unseasonal weather was due to "debris" from cold-air intrusions from the Northern Hemisphere. Whatever its cause the atmospheric depression which hung over Port of Spain for the duration of the third Test was matched by the despondency of the cricketers and the devoted and knowledgeable cricket followers of T&T.

Administrators and aficionados alike felt they were jinxed. The previous dry season rain had ruined both limited-over internationals and cost England victory and a priceless

2–0 lead in a Test series they lost 2–1 just nineteen days later. Nevertheless, such extreme disruptions at Queen's Park Oval at Test match time are considered quite out of the ordinary. Indeed, in 1976 the authorities transferred the Test match with India to Port of Spain because of torrential rain at Bourda, Georgetown. Now fun-loving Trinidadians blamed the rain on an increasing number of Guyanese immigrants. Given the spectacular events at Bourda two weeks earlier, Carl Hooper, Lance Gibbs and Clive Lloyd, to name but three, had every right to feel aggrieved. So extensive was the flooding of the ground that the local authorities, along with despairing members of the impoverished West Indies Cricket Board of Control, had no option but to reschedule the Test proceedings after only 108 minutes' play was possible on the first day and just thirty-five minutes on the second. In an attempt to breathe some life into the match and the series the teams acceded to a request to play on 8 April which was originally scheduled as the rest day. The frustrations were as acute as they were in March for the back-to-back limited-over internationals. Old-timers had time to remember how the first day of Australia's first Test at the ground on 11 April 1955 was disrupted by rain and that a crowd of 28 000 waited patiently to see Ray

Left: Aspiring cricketers at Verdant Vale near Arima, (left to right) Ganesh Ramdas (10), his brothers, Rana (8) and Devanan (9) and friend Steve Ramnasn (14). Previous pages: A passionate sentiment is expressed in this advertisement outside Queen's Park Oval.

Lindwall open the bowling to John Holt on the newly laid turf pitch.

But as was the case thirty-six years earlier, the gloom and damp could not detract from the beauty of the Queen's Park Oval. The largest and most appealing of the Test match grounds in the Caribbean, it has immense charm and is frequented by some wonderful characters. On match days it is a microcosm of Trinidad's enticing, cosmopolitan and calypsonian society despite the elitism paraded in the exclusively male members' pavilion. Standing on the fringe of the ritzy suburb of St. Clair, the Oval affords stunning views of the lush northern range which, with giant saman trees, provides an unforgettable background for a cricket canvas. And while the grandstands have limited aesthetic appeal in a city which offers such spectacular European architecture, they are warmly evocative of T&T's rich cricket traditions.

There is a stand which bears the name of the dynamic all-rounder Learie Constantine, the grandson of a slave who was feted in public life, knighted and installed the Baron Constantine of Maraval in Trinidad and Tobago and of Nelson in the County Palatine of Lancaster. Another stand revives memories of the brothers Jackie and Rolph Grant who led the West Indies in the 1930s, while a third is a monument to the fifty years' service as a player, captain, selector, and West Indies board president rendered by Jeffrey Stollmeyer.

From the upper decks of the stands

it is possible to see beyond the saman and poui trees and masses of scarlet frangipani and hibiscus to the imposing tower of Queen's Royal College, alma mater to the Port of Spain establishment and to Test

Left: Twilight zone. The stately saman tree is silhouetted against a changing sky as night envelopes the beautiful Queen's Park Oval. Above: Grin and share it. Happy youngsters at play behind a grandstand.

Queen's Royal College is an imposing example of European architecture and
numbered among the "magnificent seven buildings" which face the
Queen's Park Savannah.

cricketers Stollmeyer, Gerry Gomez and Deryck Murray. Queen's Royal College is one of the renowned "magnificent seven" buildings which stand side-by-side in Maraval Road opposite the mighty 80 ha (199 ac) Queen's Park Savannah, the biggest roundabout in the world according to taxi drivers. Port of Spain is well served for parkland and recreational ground and one of the city squares is named after Lord Harris, England's first home Test captain and eminent cricket evangelist who was born at St. Ann's in the northern range above Queen's Park Oval. Sir Pelham "Plum" Warner who captained England and was joint manager of Douglas Jardine's infamous Bodyline team to Australia in 1932–33 also was born on the island.

Limousines bearing American

Army personnel outside the Port of Spain jail holding members of the
Jamaat al Muslimeen who attempted to overthrow the government of Trinidad and
Tobago on 27 July 1990.

tourists from the cruise ships slow as they pass the "magnificent seven" and the massive pink poui near the savannah racecourse, before they head into the hills and dales of the northern range on their way to idyllic Maracas Beach. Those not constrained by a sailing schedule can continue to Las Cuevas and rugged Blanchisseuse and by way of a spectacular mountain crossing return to Port of Spain via Arima, the birthplace of Larry Gomes and Tunapuna where, as a six-year-old, the Marxist intellectual, historian and eminent writer C. L. R. James began his passionate association with cricket.

Along with the metre of calypso and the unique and triumphal sounds of the steel orchestra, cricket is an essential part of the rhythm of life of

Above: The patience of Job was required to attend the Test match. The broadsheet headlines say it all. Right: Grand colonial houses and the lush northern range form a spectacular backdrop to the largest and most appealing ground in the Caribbean.

T&T and it is played with as much fervour in the parking areas of modern shopping centres as it is on the beach and savannah and in the main streets of sleepy villages. Whereas the witty and insightful Calypsonians and master pan musicians show off their skills at Carnival, the cricket fraternity bang their drum at every Test match and limited-over international at Queen's Park Oval.

Showing disdain for the dire warnings issued by weather forecasters, hundreds of spectators arrived before dawn for the third and potentially decisive limited-over international on 10 March. Not even a soaking and a heavy 45-run loss in the abbreviated exercise the previous day had dampened their enthusiasm,

and they shared the narrow streets around the ground with churchgoers headed for 6 a.m. services — thirty minutes after the gates were opened at the Oval.

With one eye on the coin and the other on the dark clouds gathering ominously above the northern range, Border won his second toss for the series and elected to bat. Since winning the World Cup in 1987 the Australians had specialised in defending totals against all odds and the prospect of rain was not enough to make him change a highly successful method of operation. A day earlier they had been untroubled to defend 9–172 from 34 overs to become the first visiting team to win more than a solitary one-day match in the Caribbean. Now they were poised to be enshrined in history as the first

110

country to win a compressed series in the West Indies.

Stimulated by the challenge, Geoff Marsh cleverly regulated the innings with a poised 81 from 107 deliveries before he was the fifth batsman dismissed in the 42nd over. As so often is the case, he received robust support from Dean Jones who complemented his decisive 64 the previous day with a neat 36 from 49 balls. From 49 overs Australia reached a satisfactory and highly competitive 7-245 and by tearing 59 runs from his 10 overs squared the ledger with Tony Gray who had taken six wickets the day before. Their pleasure was, however, short lived and steady rain at lunch compelled umpires Clyde Cumberbatch and Lloyd Barker to again reach for their trusty calculators. They decreed the West Indies required 181 at 5.02 runs per over for 36 overs for a victory which would keep alive the series in the fourth match in Barbados where no visiting side had ever won a one-day international. Richie Richardson ensured an ignominious 3-0 defeat was averted with a daring 90 from 94 deliveries with 14 boundaries. And to the delight of his adoring supporters in the grounds, as the outer is known, Gus Logie, the captain of Trinidad and Tobago, administered the *coup de grâce* with a delightfully cheeky 24 from 21 deliveries with five boundaries.

The win was greeted with wholehearted cheers, blasts on horn and "Blue Food" Gabriel's conch shell, and with high pitched whistles which unsettled the monolithic guard dogs and their uniformed handlers.

Outside the ground, operators of the mobile sound systems officially called maxi taxis, increased the volume of the mainly mindless, sexist Dub and DJ music which announced their approach. The throbbing eight and ten-seat taxis with names such as "Passion", "Pure Energy", "Fidelity" and "Sexy Eyes" emblazoned in gilt on the windscreens provide excellent and cheap public transport but deaden the senses of the commuter.

Next to their love of Carnival, music and cricket Trinidadians and Tobagonians are passionate about

Above: That's the spirit. Drinking rum
and Coca Cola while liming on the
cycle track at Queen's Park Oval.
Left: Cover-up. Vigilant umpire Lloyd
Barker is soaked to the skin as
billowing covers are positioned at the
height of a deluge.

Left: Pan yard jam. Members of the Neal and Massy steel orchestra in full cry
in Duke Street, Port of Spain. Above: The bewitched and the braided.

liming. To lime is to relax, to hang out, to unwind, to share space with friends, to be cool, to party. At Test match time there is a ritual liming at Queen's Park Oval which brings the spirit of Carnival to cricket and another dimension to theatre in the round. If the cricket is unimaginative or unexceptional or the weather unfavourable, the entertainment provided by the many thespians in the crowd becomes the main event. And certainly the hardy and optimistic souls at the ground for the last of the three visits by the Australians were in dire need of distraction and some value for an outlay of TT$35 (A$10.83) for shelter in the enclosure and TT$12 (A$3.71) for a patch of concrete or clay behind the cycle track in the grounds.

In the Learie Constantine stand behind the bowler's arm at the northern end, Calypsonian Willard "Relator" Harris and comedian Tommy Joseph entemporised to the beat of hands on concrete and wood. At the bottom of an embankment in the grounds Edmund Joseph, the pull-string king, lured gamblers to the wobbly table under a canopy of the sort seen in any side-show alley. "Two of a kind pays three to one and five of a kind twelve to one" he barked as punters parted with their cash and waited for the wooden blocks to tumble down the tatty velvet slide and onto the table divided into squares of black, orange, blue, yellow, red and green. On a good day he will take more than TT$1000 (A$309.59). Elsewhere money changed hands over games of brag (three-card poker) and rummy, as the proletariat bemoaned the serious back injury which had befallen Ian Bishop and demanded the promotion of their left-handed prodigy Brian Lara ahead of Carl Hooper. And they drank steadily to their belief that there was a need for sweeping team changes despite the 10-wicket victory in Georgetown.

The cultural diversity of T&T is reflected in the food available from outlets in every nook and cranny of the ground. No other Test match venue in the world can offer fare ranging from cow-heel soup, pelau

Above: An uncharacteristically chipper Curtly Ambrose makes a point before a crowded Jeffrey Stollmeyer Stand. Right: All the fun of the fare. Crab and dumpling for one at a ground renowned for its cuisine.

116

(sic), fried noodles and shark sandwiches to delectable chicken, beef, potato or shrimp roti and the ubiquitous hotdog and meat pie. And to accompany such a repast there is an extensive choice of beer, spirits and fresh fruit juices to be had from bar or barrow. Heidi Hackshaw, a fashion boutique owner moonlighting in the enclosure, offered, on ice, the fresh juice of the passionfruit, cantaloupe, paw paw, tamarind, grapefruit, orange, lime and watermelon. Behind and beneath the grandstands and on the embankment, purveyors of the cricket cuisine stood by their gas bottles and spruiked for prospective customers along with those selling flags of T&T, sunglasses, multi-coloured fairy floss, iced coconuts and channa nuts. But as the days passed and the crowds

dwindled their cries became weaker. The sunglasses wallah fell silent altogether and eventually went missing.

As was the case in the first limited-over international at the ground twenty-seven days before, Vivian Richards was uncertain how to react after winning the toss. Again he returned to the pavilion for consultations before it was announced Australia would bat. Although Border would have batted on the evenly grassed but dry and cracking surface, the West Indies' decision, given their fast bowling strength, was understandable. The temperature approached 30°C (86°F) and the air was thick with moisture when Geoff Marsh and Mark Taylor went to the frontline again intoning the need to watch the ball from the hand.

The air in the Australian dressingroom and shared veiwingroom was thick with tension. The defeat at Georgetown had abruptly changed the mood of the party and the naked ambition and aggression evident throughout the one-day campaign had been replaced by a nervous uncertainty and diffidence. For their part, the selectors illustrated the extent of their dissatisfaction by discarding Mike Whitney and Greg Matthews, New South Wales teammates and kindred spirits. Despite doubts about the suitability of Bruce Reid and Stephen Waugh as replacements, the selectors

The big wet of the dry season. Rain swept down the verdant valleys of the northern range and flooded the ground on three consecutive days.

had no option but to take strong measures. Whitney had failed to take a wicket in the two Tests conceding 216 runs from 66 overs while Matthews had lost his way completely managing just three wickets at 91.00 from 73.5 overs.

While they agreed with Allan Border that negative batting had contributed to the downfall at Bourda, Geoff Marsh, Mark Taylor and David Boon were unable to redress the situation as they had hoped. Conditions favoured the pace bowlers and Curtly Ambrose bowled with menacing lift and in his fifth over dismissed Marsh (10 from 27 deliveries). Such was the skill and relentlessness of Ambrose and the persistence of Patrick Patterson that

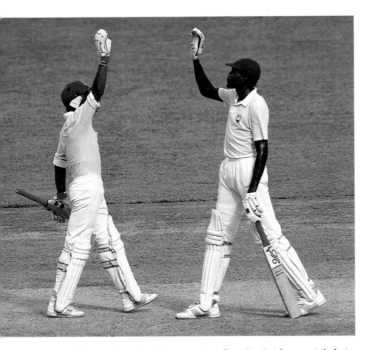

Above: Saving face again. Curtly Ambrose (right), a gangling left-hander, celebrates his first Test half century with Jeff Dujon. Right: Immersed in his work, Donovan Maynard, a member of the groundstaff, in the deep at Queen's Park Oval.

Boon needed 42 balls and 57 minutes before he scored. Taylor, who had faced 17 deliveries before he broke his duck, and Boon were spared further harassment when the rain clouds which had built up menacingly from the start dumped such a load that within an hour the ground was under water.

T&T and West Indies Board officials were dismayed and embarrassed when umpires Lloyd Barker and David Archer found that a perforated cover had caused five damp patches on the pitch at the northern end. Sensing another covers fiasco to rival Kingston, scores of journalists, commentators and supporters trooped on to the sodden ground to make an assessment. It was an invasion which went unnoticed by the ground authorities but not by Tony Cozier, the international voice of West Indies cricket. "An assorted cast of dozens — Australian players and officials joined by journalists, TV personnel, and, for all anyone knew or cared, casual tourists, nut sellers, grave diggers and city vagrants — came out to walk on, push and prod the area of the ground that, above all others, used to be sacrosanct. Now it was as busy a thoroughfare as adjoining Tragarete Road without the slightest sign of security," he wrote in his syndicated despatch to the *Daily Nation* in Barbados. Given the extent of his disappointment in Jamaica, Allan Border accepted the misadventure with remarkably good grace and publicly called on the International Cricket Council to standardise pitch covering at Test

Sunday at Sobo Village. Gus and Lisa Logie on the veranda of the house in which he was born the youngest of 10 children in September 1960.

For two years she had fought against a severe heart condition which at times had seen her confined to a nursing home for intensive treatment. By the time the first Test match started at Sabina Park on 1 March she had lapsed into unconsciousness and mercifully never knew her son was poleaxed when he attempted to hook against Craig McDermott. From the time he first played on the savannah she had constantly worried about his being trampled by bigger and stronger boys. But time and again he quietly allayed her fears, uncomplainingly took the hard knocks and developed a mental and moral strength that was to help make him a famous son of Trinidad and Tobago. "I came four years after a sister when all the other children were spaced two years apart. So there was always this joke that I wasn't to be. But I always said to her that I was a godsend."

By the time he was born on 28 September 1960 only four of his siblings were still at Foxhole, as the locals have long called Priddie Lane on account of its shape. His father, Peter, died when he was nine and by fifteen he was the only male in the house and his bond with Augustina grew stronger still.

"She really was like a mother and father; everything to me. She nurtured me in the way she wanted me to go, although she was never one to insist that I do things she wanted me to do. She would influence me to do what she regarded as the right things. She would tell me that life holds no guarantees but she was always encouraging and was always one to lend support when you needed it most. I felt I lost more than a mum. I lost a friend, a companion, someone I could also trust, someone I could always confide in. In good and bad times she was always there for me."

At the age of ten he promised his mother he would use his cricket bat to protect her from any evil. Already the cricket bat was a powerful symbol in his life.

From his earliest sorties on to the savannah and into the playground at Le Brea Roman Catholic primary school it was evident Logie had been blessed with a special talent; perhaps a gift from God. His body was small but it was not brittle and his speed, poise and co-ordination helped him compensate for a lack of strength and power. He was a natural sportsman adept at cricket, soccer, athletics and table tennis. When he realised cricket was of such importance that schoolchildren were granted a holiday on the opening day of a Test match, there was no question it would be his preferred game.

As with so many children throughout the Caribbean his first bat was fashioned from the frond of a coconut palm and the ball was a breadfruit. Word of his prowess as a batsman spread quickly through the village, and as a test of his suitability to play with the bigger boys on the savannah, he was given a bat crudely constructed from board to combat demon bowlers armed with a ball of hard pitch.

Between the village of Sobo and the town of La Brea lies Pitch Lake, a strange, shifting morass from which vast quantities of high quality bitumen have been mined since its discoverer, Sir Walter Raleigh, caulked his ships in 1595. Apparently oblivious to the legend that the lake once devoured a tribe of Chayma Indians as punishment for eating hummingbirds in which the souls of their ancestors reposed, Logie and his friends played on the lake and moulded asphalt into balls for cricket. After learning to cope with the peculiar black missile, the transition to sponge ball and the conventional hard ball was relatively easy. And by then he had won acceptance from the bigger boys and had been entrusted with a hand-me-down bat which looked like the genuine article used in Test matches.

Logie loved the country and the friendliness of village life but at Test match time regretted Sobo was 80 km (50 miles) and a long, tiring and expensive journey away from beautiful Queen's Park Oval in Port of Spain. Unable to travel to the capital he depended on radio and television commentators to transport him to his magic world. He would sit for hours beside the radio at Foxhole or before the black and white television receiver at a friend's home. Only two television sets were to be found in Sobo in the early 1970s and there was a ritual gathering of villagers whenever a Test match was televised.

By the time Ian Chappell's Australian team achieved their heroic 2-0 success in the West Indies in 1973, Logie had decided to pursue a career as a cricketer. Unlike his four brothers he had no inclination to work in the oil industry as his father had done.

"Somehow I felt that I wanted to be different. I had a dream; a desire to do something different and I pursued it. I felt I wanted to become a Test cricketer. I wanted to travel the world, meet different people and experience different lifestyles. It was a determination, a desire to get to the top."

The mental toughness and physical hardness developed on the savannah served him well and at the age of thirteen he was chosen to play his first club game for Texaco-Brighton (now Trintoc-Brighton) at La Brea. At once he was required to match wits with established first-class players and confronted unorthodox left-arm spinner, Inshan Ali, and Raphick Jumadeen, a slow left-arm orthodox bowler who had both played for the West Indies against Chappell's tourists in 1973.

Under the watchful eye of his noted coach and friend William Guadeloupe, Logie paid greater attention to his batting and fielding and earned impressive notices as a regular member of the country's youth teams. At the same time influential people within the cricket community raised his hackles by loudly pointing out the difficulty he would have reaching the Trinidad and Tobago team from an obscure village in the south of the island. It would be to his advantage, they suggested, if he moved to Port of Spain and entered the society which traditionally provided the country's Test cricketers. A proud and intelligent teenager with a strong sense of social justice, he railed against the overbearing presumptuousness of the establishment. As a junior clerk in a credit union office in the nearby village of Vessigny he vowed to defy the odds and play

The casual street and savannah cricketers of Sobo Village pose proudly with their celebrated clansman Gus Logie.

for Trinidad and Tobago from the family home in what the ruling class mockingly referred to as the "Deep South".

"There was a lot of negative feedback and people would say you can only make the Trinidad team if you are Mr so-and-so's son and you are in Port of Spain. But nothing was going to stop me and I wouldn't let the negative people around me or the negative talk influence me in any way. I didn't see why I should have to leave my home and go somewhere else to make it. The determination to make it against all odds was uppermost in my mind. I felt if I did it I would encourage others to do it."

Logie's unwavering faith in his ability was rewarded in April 1979 when he was chosen to play for Trinidad and Tobago against the Combined Islands at Queen's Park Oval. It was a rare event to be chosen for the country without having first appeared in a first division club game and Augustina Logie and the extended family of Sobo rejoiced in his heady success. Four years later the community again exploded with pride when he was drafted into the formidably powerful West Indies team for the first Test match with India at Sabina Park. In the fourth match of the series

at Bridgetown, Barbados, he scored his maiden Test century batting at number five ahead of Clive Lloyd.

By the time the 1980s gave way to the 1990s Logie had grown in stature as an international cricketer proving a consistently productive number six batsman, a courageous and clever catcher at short leg and a brilliant out fieldsman. In recognition of his accomplishments and, no doubt, of his engaging personality, gentle nature and strong sense of fairness, the Port of Spain establishment awarded him the captaincy of Trinidad and Tobago in 1990-91. It was the crowning glory for a man who stands so tall at 165 cm (5 ft 5 in).

On 9 April, the fourth day of the rain-ruined third Test match at Queen's Park Oval, Lisa Logie (nee Hyacinth), his childhood sweetheart from the other side of the Independent Baptist Church in Sobo, gave birth to a 2.2 kg (4 lb 14 oz) son.

When he is old enough to run on the savannah and play with a ball made of pitch, Giovan Gustine Logie will learn of the love, strength and faith of the grandmother he never knew.

And his bond with Augustine will grow stronger still.

considerable anxiety. Nearly seventy-two hours later the pitch had been deadened by the torrential rain and the ball did not come on to the bat at all. Until an uncharacteristic rush of blood brought about his downfall after four hours, he had set a shining example.

But of his colleagues only Mark Waugh showed comparable resourcefulness against intelligent bowling designed to exploit the conditions and the discomfort of the Australians. Led by Courtney Walsh, whose place in the team had been threatened by Ezra Moseley and Tony Gray, each of the bowlers, off-spinner Carl Hooper included, worked with unerring accuracy and cleverly varied their length. They wore down Allan Border (43 from 145 balls in 222 minutes without a boundary) and Dean Jones (21 from 75 balls in 123 minutes) and in 90 overs in 6 hours and 40 minutes Australia advanced their score by just 204 runs. Such was the tedium that considerably more attention was paid to "Relator" Harris's stinging observations and poetry and to Tommy Joseph's gags.

The Test match was not, however, to die without one last and spectacular convulsion. As critics near and far began to administer the last rites, the fast bowlers, despite the slowness of the pitch, contrived to give it the kiss-of-life and suddenly, inexplicably, 12 wickets fell for 235.

The extraordinary procession was started by another weak-kneed withdrawal by the Australian middle and late order batsmen, notably Craig McDermott and Merv Hughes whose immediate future had been

scrutinised at selection. Discredited in Kingston and Georgetown they surrendered again and Border watched in utter disbelief as the last four wickets fell for one run in nine deliveries with McDermott and Hughes failing to score — Hughes for the third time in as many innings. So the Australian innings which began at 10.05 a.m. on Friday 5 April concluded at 10.55 a.m. on Tuesday 9

126

April — 294 runs agonisingly accumulated from 128.1 overs in 9 hours and 40 minutes.

Intent on atoning for such timidity and ineptitude at the crease, McDermott and Hughes wrought havoc and for one fleeting, fantastic moment it seemed the West Indies would not reach the modest 95 required to avoid the follow-on. Introduced to the attack in the 15th

Balcony scene. Dean Jones (left) and Allan Border in pensive mood in the players' viewing area during the rain-ruined Test match.

over and following a solitary over from Allan Border in his role as the frontline slow bowler, Hughes launched a stunning assault against a succession of batsmen who played as though they had long before established an unassailable lead in

TWIN ACHIEVEMENTS

Not even torrential downpours day after day rained on the parade of Stephen and Mark Waugh at Queen's Park Oval.

Four minutes apart at birth, at the age of twenty-five they became the first twin brothers to play Test cricket when Stephen was reinstated to the Australian team after the inglorious events of Georgetown.

While their precociousness as cricketers has given them a shared identity they are vastly different in look, personality, temperament, and attitude, and to the casual observer appear to be a world apart.

As with Ian and Greg Chappell, the only other brothers to have played Test cricket together for Australia in the twentieth century, competitive-ness was as important as camaraderie as they grew and sought admission to the brotherhood of cricket's elite.

Assertive cricketers by instinct, they are essentially undemonstrative, if ambitious men. But where there is a brooding intensity about Stephen, the first born, there is an irreverent casualness about Mark. Initially it was thought Stephen would benefit from his thoughtfulness and seriousness and that Mark would be disadvantaged by his haphazardness and happy detachment. But by the summer of 1990-91 observers and critics were tending towards the view that the absolute reverse was the case.

While they are not tactile or overtly emotional as brothers they have, they assure the inquisitive, feelings for each other that transcend their steely professionalism as cricketers.

As speculation mounted to the likely composition of the team, Mark quietly sought confirma-

Stephen (left) and Mark Waugh, the first twins to play Test cricket and, with Ian and Greg Chappell, the only brothers to have played Test cricket together for Australia in the twentieth century.

tion from Patrick Smithers, a fine young Australian journalist covering the tour, that no twins had ever played in a Test match. Clearly he was enthralled at the prospect of being a part of the game's rich history. Stephen, who has always taken a close interest in the game's history and memorabilia, would have known the answer and furthermore probably could have identified the four pairs of brothers who played for Australia in the nineteenth century.

In the first Test match in March 1877 Dave Gregory led Australia to a 45-run victory while his brother Ned, in his only appearance, had the ignominious distinction of scoring Test cricket's first duck. Two years later Alec Bannerman's first Test coincided with the last played by his elder brother Charles, who scored Test cricket's first century, while the incomparable George Giffen was joined by his younger brother Walter for two Test matches in 1891-92 and in 1894-95 Albert and Harry Trott played three times together.

It was not until the Chappells pooled their priceless resources against Pakistan at Adelaide in December 1972 that Australian brothers played against a country other than England. It was the eleventh of their forty-three appearances together between December 1970 and February 1980, and Ian marked the occasion with his highest Test score of 196. Appropriately they were both in Port of Spain as members of the media and shared the excitement of the moment.

Much to the pleasure of the small crowd watching Australia's painstaking progression, fate determined that the brothers should bat together on such an auspicious occasion. When Allan Border was brilliantly run out by Carl Hooper, Stephen, who had been preferred to Greg Matthews at number seven, strode to the middle to join Mark. They kept to themselves any feelings of pride and satisfaction at their accomplishment and without ceremony added fifty-eight in ninety minutes before Stephen drove eagerly at Courtney Walsh and was caught at the wicket by Jeff Dujon. Stephen contributed twenty-six from fifty four deliveries in ninety minutes but as had been the case since the team reached the Caribbean the attention of pundits and commentators was focused on his brother.

Although he first played alongside Stephen for Australia in a limited-over match against Pakistan in December 1988, Mark had to wait patiently for another twenty-five months before he was chosen for his first Test match against England at Adelaide. And when his promotion finally came it was at the expense of his brother who had been propelled into Test cricket against India on Boxing Day 1985 at the age of twenty after scoring two centuries in eleven first-class matches. Mark who had waited in the wings for 100 first-class matches and scored twenty-five hundreds rejoiced with a glorious maiden century in four minutes shy of three hours. Stephen, reared when Australian cricket had fallen on hard times, took forty-two innings in twenty-seven Tests and three-and-a-half years to score his first century.

While Mark had not produced such consummate strokeplay against the infinitely superior West Indies attack he had, nevertheless, displayed exceptional poise and touch, and from the outset won impressive reviews wherever he played. During the second Test in Guyana Clive Lloyd unequivocally declared Mark to be the finest leg-side player in the world.

Although he was dropped twice at Port of Spain he showed considerable maturity to adapt to the slowness of the pitch and maintained his impressive consistency by top-scoring with sixty-four from 178 deliveries in 201 minutes.

The following morning, in his widely syndicated column in the *Trinidad Guardian* Lloyd wrote: "Every time I see Mark Waugh I think I am seeing someone special. He has a very uncomplicated stance and has a lot of time to play the ball, like all the great players I've had the privilege of seeing.

"Australia must be delighted to have found such a young and exciting player who is maturing with every innings he plays. I am positive that Mark will provide lots of enjoyment to cricket lovers. His talent is rare and we shall be hearing much more about him in the future."

the series. Carl Hooper, Gus Logie and Vivian Richards fell in quick succession and at 5–56 in the 21st over the West Indies were in dire straits and the faithful few suddenly lost interest in peripheral entertainments and were transfixed by the remarkable events in the middle. Richie Richardson and Jeff Dujon reacted to the crisis in the time-honoured fashion of the Caribbean cricketer by lashing 30 runs in four overs, each run galling Dean Jones who missed a straight forward catch offered by Richardson against Bruce Reid when he was 16.

Hughes weathered the flurry and had Richardson brilliantly caught at slip by Mark Taylor to see the West Indies 6–86.

But for all the excitement of his four wickets for just 19 runs from 5.3 overs Hughes was not able to turn the screws. And nor could McDermott or Reid, and as was the case at Sabina Park in the first Test, Jeff Dujon and Curtly Ambrose organised an impressive resistance operation. In Kingston they had hauled their colleagues from the bloody mire of 6–75 with a seventh wicket stand of 69 in 72 minutes. On this occasion they

THIRD TEST

at Queen's Park Oval, Port of Spain 5, 6, 8, 9, 10 April — West Indies won toss

AUSTRALIA

			Min	Balls	4s			Min	Balls	4s
G. Marsh	c Hooper b Ambrose	10	38	27	1	lbw b Marshall	12	85	49	1
M. Taylor	c Walsh b Marshall	61	241	147	9	b Patterson	2	7	9	—
D. Boon	c Logie b Patterson	27	173	111	3	b Walsh	29	97	68	4
A. Border	run out	43	222	145	—	not out	27	125	78	3
D. Jones	lbw b Patterson	21	123	75	3	not out	39	145	118	3
M. Waugh	lbw b Marshall	64	201	178	3					
S. Waugh	c Dujon b Walsh	26	90	54	2					
I. Healy	c Dujon b Marshall	9	61	31	1					
C. McDermott	c Richardson b Patterson	0	5	3	—					
M. Hughes	lbw b Patterson	0	2	3	—					
B. Reid	not out	0	2	—	—					
Sundries	(6B, 14LB, 13NB)		33			Sundries (1B, 9LB, 4NB)		14		
Total			294			Three wickets for		123		

Fall: 24 (Marsh), 93 (Boon), 116 (Taylor), 174 (Jones), 210 (Border), 268 (S. Waugh), 293 (M. Waugh), 294 (McDermott), 294 (Hughes), 294 (Healy).

Fall: 3 (Taylor), 49 (Marsh), 53 (Boon).

	O	M	R	W		O	M	R	W
Ambrose	29	7	51	1		10	4	11	—
Patterson	26	2	50	4		7	—	27	1
Marshall	18.1	3	55	3		10	3	24	1
Walsh	30	9	45	1		12	6	11	1
Hooper	25	5	73	—		13	3	38	—
Richardson						1	—	2	—

Batting Time: 630 Min. Overs: 128.1

Batting Time: 232 Min. Overs: 53

contributed 87 in 124 minutes for the eighth wicket and Ambrose, a gangling left-hander with a good eye and batting pretensions, gained the satisfaction of scoring his first half-century in his 26th Test. Certainly it was with a practised flourish that he raised his bat to acknowledge the applause from his relieved colleagues standing on the pavilion balcony. While struggling to regain full confidence with the gloves, Dujon regained form and favour as a batsman with a well-crafted 70, his second half-century for the series and his highest Test score since his fifth

Test century against Pakistan at the same ground three years earlier.

A calm man and temperate shop steward, he had batted for 4 hours and 10 minutes to uphold the pride of West Indies cricket. It was a stirring innings and one which deservedly won him the Man of the Match award.

The northern range was bathed in sunlight as Dujon was presented with his trophy and the Australians were regaled with dark stories of the fate which awaited them in Barbados and Antigua. The weather gods had had their way.

WEST INDIES

			Min	Balls	4s
G. Greenidge	c M. Waugh b Reid	12	25	15	2
D. Haynes	b McDermott	1	19	15	—
R. Richardson	c Taylor b Hughes	30	92	63	5
C. Hooper	lbw b Hughes	12	38	32	2
G. Logie	c M. Waugh b Hughes	1	14	10	—
V. Richards	c S. Waugh b Hughes	2	8	6	—
J. Dujon	lbw b McDermott	70	179	250	6
M. Marshall	c McDermott b Border	12	34	28	2
C. Ambrose	c Border b M. Waugh	53	124	110	6
C. Walsh	not out	12	76	52	—
P. Patterson	b McDermott	0	6	11	—
Sundries	(6B, 7LB, 9NB)	22			
Total		227			

Fall: 16 (Haynes), 18 (Greenidge), 46 (Hooper), 52 (Logie), 56 (Richards), 86 (Richardson), 110 (Marshall), 197 (Ambrose), 225 (Dujon), 227 (Patterson).

	O	M	R	W
McDermott	14.2	2	36	3
Reid	22	—	79	1
Border	19	5	28	1
Hughes	17	5	48	4
S. Waugh	5	—	10	—
M. Waugh	6	2	9	1
Jones	1	—	4	—

Batting Time: 355 Min. Overs: 84.2

Match drawn

Man of the Match: J. Dujon. Umpires: L. Barker & D. Archer. 12th Men: P. Taylor (Aust.), B. Lara (W. Ind.). Rain washed out play — 6 April.

CHAPTER FIVE

TO THE BEAT OF THE BAJAN DRUM

Barbados and the Fourth Test
Kensington Oval ● 19-24 April 1991

A SIXTH SENSE BORN OF SIX YEARS'
hard labour as captain forewarned Allan
Border of impending doom in the heartland of
West Indies cricket. His uneasiness had grown
steadily since the frustrations of sodden

Trinidad and as preparations intensified for the decisive fourth Test at Kensington Oval he was cold with apprehension in the heat.

Since his maturity as a captain he has been more aware of subtle changes of mood, attitude and opinion and prepared to trust his instincts. As team officials made all the optimistic noises expected of them before a main event, Border asked his players to cancel external social arrangements and spend the time together. Three days before the Test match he spirited them away from

their soulless resort to an inn for group therapy of the kind made fashionable by his mentor Ian Chappell twenty years earlier. He felt his men were losing their way and was anxious to reinforce the sense of family which had served the team so well since the World Cup triumph of 1987.

The incessant rain had robbed the tour of a rhythm and dampened enthusiasm when it was most needed. A month earlier the team had swept across the island on a wave of success created by the historic win in a limited-over international at Kensington Oval and a one-day competition in the Caribbean. But the euphoria of that moment was long forgotten and the freshness and buoyancy overtaken by a tiredness and despondency. Furthermore, Barbados, its population of 250 000 swollen by many hundreds of cricket supporters from Australia, England and Bermuda, provided First World distractions near the end of a three-month tour and a seven-month season. History had taught Border and his close friends and loyal lieutenants, Geoff Marsh and David Boon, to watch closely for signs of physical and mental fatigue during the last two weeks of a tour when the team was most likely to self-destruct.

Given the West Indies' remarkable record at Kensington Oval, Border understood it would take an optimum performance to be competitive. The West Indies had won their previous nine Tests at the ground and indeed had lost there only once, by four wickets on a sticky pitch to Bob Wyatt's England tourists in January

Previous pages: Island idyll. Coral shores at sunset. Left: Route bound. Perhaps
the simplest public transport system in the world: "Out of City" and "To City"
Above: Apres-jet ski. Windell Ellis of the Bajan new wave.

The quaint and distinctively Barbadian chattel house.

1935 in the first Test won against a second innings declaration. The only comfort for the Australians was the knowledge that in all probability the pitch would provide pace and even bounce. Certainly that had been the case in the decisive limited-over match a month earlier when Marsh had played with aplomb for a record eighth century and Border with a freedom of summers long past for a thrilling seventy-nine from eighty-seven deliveries.

Like Ian Johnson, Bob Simpson, Ian Chappell and Kim Hughes before him, Border dreamed of devising the formula to win at Kensington Oval. He had won his two Test matches as captain at Lord's, had held aloft the World Cup at Eden Gardens and, in addition to some significant limited-over successes, overcame a bold

challenge by Pakistan at the Melbourne Cricket Ground. Victory against the odds at Kensington Oval would complete an imposing list of achievements at the world's foremost cricket grounds.

In contrast to the other renowned venues Kensington Oval is small, as though built to scale for a country of just 426 km^2 (164½ sq. miles). It is a charming, intimate place with a quaintness which reflects the country's proud British heritage.

Unlike the rest of the region, Barbados, the most easterly of the curved chain of Caribbean islands, was neither discovered by Christopher Columbus nor occupied by more than one power. Until its independence in 1966 it had been exclusively British territory since 1625. From the little stone cottages

Field of memories. Velda Thornhill, a woman of dignity and bearing, reflects on 25 years as a sugarcane cutter.

which open on to narrow, winding lanes to the architecture and statuary of the bustling and welcoming capital of Bridgetown, the Englishness is inescapable. Only along the beautiful palm-fringed beaches of the western coastline and in the country where fields of sugar cane are broken by clusters of gaily painted and chattel houses, does the island assume a Caribbean identity.

Thin and generally broken roads criss-cross the island and passengers from cruise ships pausing in the deep water harbour take to the Mini Mokes which swarm about the island like migrating locusts. The country is just 33 km (20½ miles) long and 22 km (13½ miles) wide and can be seen in a day, navigating not by a map, but by the bus signs which simply state "Out of City" and "To City". A sweep

of the west coast resorts, hotels and guest houses cum sanitariums provides ample evidence that tourism has supplanted sugar as the country's principal industry and provides employment for 25 per cent of the work force. But unlike Antigua, Barbados has not abandoned its sugar crops and closed its factories, and a journey east to the comparatively rugged and windswept Atlantic coast is made by way of the most abundant fields. After harvesting by either machine or machete the fields are turned over for the planting of yams, potatoes, carrots and beans.

The country's fascination for cricket was born out of the strength of the bonds with England and historians believe the game was first played by British military officers stationed at the Garrison Savannah just south of Bridgetown in the eighteenth century. Appropriately, it was at the 20 ha (49½ ac) Savannah in February 1975 that Garfield St. Aubrun Sobers, arguably the most famous Bajan of all, was knighted for his services to the game. That a country with a population of barely a quarter of a million people can consistently produce the game's most eminent cricketers is a phenomenon of world sport. A crescent of grandstands at the northern end of Kensington Oval bears testimony to the extraordinary richness of the island's cricket heritage and its unique contribution to the international game. To the east of the Pickwick Pavilion lies the Sir Garfield Sobers pavilion and a three-tier structure dedicated to the incomparable fast bowlers Wesley Hall and Charlie Griffith. To the west is a stand which keeps alive the name of George Challenor, the first West Indian master batsman who was known as "Lord Runs-come" to his many admirers. Alongside it is the 3Ws stand and annexe — monuments which commemorate the exceptional deeds of Sir Frank Worrell, Everton Weekes and Clyde Walcott. And for good measure there are gates which have been named after John Goddard who was captain in twenty-two of his twenty-seven Tests and Herman Griffith the first of the distinguished Barbadian fast bowlers.

At Lord's, the autograph seekers, stargazers and paparazzi habitually gather near the Grace Gates. At the Melbourne Cricket Ground they pace the southern fringe of Yarra Park and

AN INCOMPARABLE TRINITY

From the green hill where Frank Worrell is buried you can see where the sky meets the Caribbean Sea and hear the howl of the winds of change.

Sir Frank Mortimore Maglinne Worrell, the spirit of cricket between Australia and the West Indies, died of leukemia at the age of forty-two and was laid to rest on the Barbados campus of the University of the West Indies he served with distinction in Jamaica and Trinidad.

In effect, his simple grave at Cave Hill, a few minutes drive north of his native Bridgetown, is a shrine. Each year cricket people come from near and far to pay respect to a consummate cricketer, a statesman and philosopher and the first black man to lead the West Indies on tour — to Australia for the watershed series of 1960-61. The grave is set in a field of crotons, and benches have been recessed into a retaining wall so visitors can rest and contemplate.

Worrell's memory is perpetuated by The Frank Worrell Trophy for Test match competition between the West Indies and Australia, by his portrait on the Barbados five dollar bill and by "The Three Ws" grandstand and annexe at Kensington Oval.

The legend of the three Ws was born in the 1950s when the extraordinary batting exploits of Worrell, Everton De Courcey Weekes and Clyde Leopold Walcott captured the imagination of the world.

As they had done periodically since they buried their mate in 1967 Weekes and Walcott made their way to Worrell's grave on the rest day of the Test match.

Weekes: "It can be very emotional. We got on so well together the three of us. It is very difficult, even at this stage, to separate Frank from us."

Walcott: "Every time you come here or somebody talks about Frank you recall within yourself memories of situations we had when we were all together."

Weekes: "And they are very precious memories. He was such a fine person."

Walcott: "On tour we socialised together; we did everything together."

They were in nostalgic mood as they perched on the retaining wall. The passing summers had not dulled their senses or their memories; or their abiding love for their friend.

Walcott: "It is difficult to take someone out of their time but Frank would have been a great player in any era. He would have adapted to the day. But I don't know whether he could have worn a helmet. I can't think I would have worn a helmet."

Weekes: "You didn't even wear a thigh pad. You just had a towel in your pocket. I'm certain I wouldn't have worn a helmet because the boots were too heavy in the first place!"

They laughed unselfconsciously at their reminiscences and Weekes told his mates of a recent telephone call from the Australian all-rounder and bon vivant Keith Miller and how they had scoffed at the regalia which adorns the contemporary player.

Weekes, who was born in February 1925, six months after Worrell, divides his time between New York and Barbados and was at Kensington Oval to provide expert analysis of the Test match for radio. Walcott, by eleven months the youngest of the triumvirate, entertained a host of dignitaries in his capacity as president of the West Indies Cricket Board of Control (WICBC).

While cold statistics tell nothing of the personality of the three Ws' batting, their records, nevertheless, beg telling. In 48 Test matches Weekes amassed 4455 runs with 15 hundreds at 58.61 while Walcott averaged 56.68 in accumulating 3798 runs with 15 centuries in 44 appearances.

Worrell, who won nine of his 15 Tests as captain (losing three, drawing two and tieing one) scored 3860 runs at 49.48 with nine centuries in 51 Tests between 1948 and 1963. Furthermore, he took 69 wickets at 38.73 and 43 catches.

In his obituary to Sir Frank in the 1968 *Wisden Cricketers' Almanack,* Sir Learie Constantine wrote: "Sir Neville Cardus has written of Sir Frank that he never made a crude or an ungrammatical stroke. I agree with that. While Walcott bludgeoned the bowlers and Weekes dominated them, the stylist Worrell waved them away. There

The legend of the 3Ws. Clyde Walcott (left) and Everton Weekes at the grave of their friend Frank Worrell at Cave Hill.

was none of the savage aggression of a Sobers in his batting. He was the artist. All three Ws were geniuses but Worrell was my favourite because he had more style and elegance."

In February 1991 Lady Worrell was buried alongside her husband on the green hill as the winds of change growled and the WICBC intensified a hunt for The Frank Worrell Trophy which inexplicably and inexcusably had gone missing.

toss, the Australians routed the West Indies for 149 — their lowest score in thirty-three Tests against Australia since 1975 and their most meagre return against all comers in the Caribbean since Ian Chappell's visitors in 1972–73. Given traditional trends at the ground Allan Border's decision to send the West Indies into bat was not surprising. Indeed, the last captain to bat first after winning the toss was Pakistan's Mushtaq Mohammed in 1976–77. But to invite the hosts to bat after choosing only three specialist bowlers defied all logic.

But Allan Border, who rightfully has the loudest voice at selection, was unrepentant. After careful consideration he became convinced that the combined resources of Mark and Stephen Waugh represented a more potent force than did Terry Alderman who had been so sadly out of touch since falling ill at the start of the tour. While Alderman had only modest claims to promotion, his effort against a West Indies Board XI just days before the Test suggested that Kensington Oval at last provided a platform from which he could perform. Certainly in the minds of most pundits he had entered calculations by taking 5–40 during the damp skirmish mostly remembered for Dean Jones drawing attention to Keith Arthurton's oversized bat. And unquestionably he needed an opportunity to justify his passage after a tour mostly spent behind sunglasses on viewing balconies.

The dangers of entering a Test match at Kensington Oval with an attack known to be unbalanced or impotent should have been well known to the Australians. In the nine Tests played since Mushtaq's visit, the captain winning the toss had elected to bowl first. For the West Indies the tactic had been a resounding success with six victories from as many attempts. But for England captains Ian Botham, David Gower and Allan Lamb the strategy had failed and resulted in defeat. But Border's mind was made up. In essence he did not have sufficient confidence in his batsmen and paid scant regard to the assurances from Barbados Cricket Association officials and groundstaff that the pitch was chock full of runs and would be noticeably quicker on the second day.

He was relieved rather than self-satisfied at the unexpected success of his three bowlers who completed the coup in 4 hours and 39 minutes. The West Indians were disconcerted by the slowness of the pitch and only Desmond Haynes and Viv Richards showed a preparedness to build an innings and reached 20. Brought together at 3–22 in the 14th over they played with great restraint and patience particularly against Craig McDermott who bowled an inordinate number of short-pitched deliveries. But McDermott's bouncer barrage was not as mindless or futile as it seemed. In time he lured Richards into the hook and had him caught deep behind square leg by Merv Hughes just as he had done at Sabina Park. His demise precipitated a collapse which not even the resolute but irritable Haynes could prevent

On the warpath. Excited by the bounce on offer, Craig McDermott had spring in his
step as he swept into his delivery stride past Viv Richards.

and the last seven wickets fell for 77 runs in 27 overs.

In a considerable exercise of self-denial "Des-man", as Haynes is warmly known to his legion of home fans, faced 134 deliveries in 212 minutes for just 28 runs — 12 of them coming in three scoring shots. He lived on his nerves throughout the innings and momentarily lost his self-control when taunted by wicketkeeper Ian Healy. Having sweated and scraped to reach 10 in 17 overs Haynes was upset by what he regarded as a frivolous and needlessly provocative appeal by Healy as he matched wits with the rampant Craig McDermott. Healy and his colleagues in the cordon were agitated by Haynes indicating that the ball had deflected from his shirt when they genuinely believed it had struck his bat. Haynes stunned the capacity house of 12 500 when he removed his helmet and walked towards Healy waving his bat menacingly. Healy responded by blowing him a kiss as Richards ambled down the pitch and touched gloves with Haynes in a powerful show of solidarity.

Moments later Haynes complained of grit in his right eye and motioned to David Boon at shortleg to assist him. Boon made a point of remaining unmoved and Richards again came to the aid of his deputy. Haynes continued to seethe and he exchanged more words with Healy as they left the ground for lunch. The following day Haynes, a holder of his country's Silver Crown of Merit, made a public apology to his admirers but not to Healy. In an interview published in the *Barbados Sunday Sun*, Haynes said: "Healy used abusive language to me and I am sorry it looked as though I was protesting because he appealed. It was just a matter of me showing Healy where the ball hit me on my shirt but then he started cursing me. It was not that I was trying in any way to make a scene and I apologise to the fans and people of Barbados." The unseemly incidents provided further evidence of the extreme change in on-field attitude

Left: Merv Hughes (1-125) played the entertainer while Gordon Greenidge (226) played the game. Geoff Marsh (far left) looked for the ball while Allan Border (alongside wicketkeeper Ian Healy) searched for inspiration. Above: Provocative Desmond Haynes can elicit neither assistance nor sympathy from David Boon.

and demeanour by both Healy and Haynes over the previous year.

Such was the ineptitude of the batting that a crowd renowned for being lively, loud and loving as well as formidably knowledgeable and patriotic, fell silent. Ironically, just a month earlier the Barbados Cricket Association (BCA) fleetingly took leave of its senses and attempted to legislate for silence at the decisive limited-over international. Claiming they were compelled to act on complaints of noise pollution received from players and supporters during the England tour the previous year, the BCA moved to stop the beat of the Bajan drums by banning drums, cymbals, trumpets and any other musical instrument.

The community railed against the high-handedness and vented its spleen in calls to talk-back radio programs and in letters to the editors of the *Daily Nation* and *The Advocate*. The *Daily Nation* ran a biting editorial headlined "BCA playing down the wrong line" and MacDonald (Mac) Fingall, a noted Calypsonian, comedian, MC and social activist, called on Bajans to boycott the match. Within twenty-four hours the BCA had no option but to reverse its decision and ask patrons to use "their good sense and discretion to control the noise level" and Fingall was given a special ovation when he arrived to blow his trumpet with the Kensington Posse. Nevertheless the authorities went ahead and printed a provocative notice on the back of all Test match tickets: "Musical instruments, drums, cymbals, radio (without headphones)

One face of patriotism. Thousands of visitors from Australia, England and Bermuda were intoxicated by the unique atmosphere of Kensington Oval.

wicket of them all Marshall succeeded in sowing the seed of doubt in the minds of the batsmen who were to follow. And yet again the middle and late order did not have the heart for the fight and after just 4 hours and 26 minutes Australia were dismissed for 134 — their last seven wickets falling for 39 runs in 14.2 overs. It was a humiliating collapse which made a nonsense of the claim that the top six was the country's finest for 20 years. It was patently clear that against bowling of the highest calibre the Australians remained heavily reliant on their seasoned leader.

Curtly Ambrose, Patrick Patterson, Malcolm Marshall and Courtney Walsh ruthlessly completed the task in 50.1 overs, Walsh taking 4–14 from 5.1 overs to lift beyond 150 his aggregate of wickets in 44 Test matches.

Bajans are devoted to Test cricket and each morning, by seven o'clock, hundreds of spectators were milling around outside the ground particularly near the lyric theatre which is the Kensington grandstand. The sense of excitement was infectious and hundreds of animated followers queued at the narrow entrances to the stand oblivious of the signs which warned: "Overcrowding can be dangerous. Help us to control illegal overcrowding."

Apparently on this occasion the overcrowding was legal and Mac Fingall, his grandmother's potion at the ready, and King Dyal, in candy-striped suit and shocking pink gloves, had to pick their way through a mass of deliriously happy supporters to take their positions. At Fingall's direction the band comprising trumpet, cymbals, drums, whistles and conch rang out its support, reaching a high pitch as the bowler returned to his mark. In deference to the batsmen, Fingall, with the flourish of the maestro, stopped the music as the bowler moved into his delivery stride; cacophany being replaced by a conspiratorial silence. Much to the agitation of his subjects, King Dyal proclaimed the music should be stopped altogether.

At the start of the West Indies' innings, photographers with a sense of history positioned themselves strategically to record the entrance of Gordon Greenidge and Desmond Haynes. Given that Greenidge had scored just 91 runs at 15.16 in the series and was 11 days away from his 40th birthday it was thought likely he was playing his last Test match and that the greatest opening combination in contemporary cricket was to end. By the end of the day the "shooters", along with everyone else at the ground, hastily revised their opinion as Greenidge and Haynes celebrated their 16th century opening partnership in Test matches. Furthermore, Greenidge remained unconquered just 15 runs away from his 19th Test century.

The pain Border experienced from his cracked left thumb was substantially overtaken by the agony of watching the humiliation of his colleagues from the tiered balcony in front of the shuttered dressingroom in the Sir Garfield Sobers pavilion. Without access to a spinner and a fourth fast-medium bowler, his deputy

Averting the mid-life crisis. Within two weeks of his 40th birthday Gordon Greenidge rediscovered the joy of impetuous youth and batted for 11 hours and 17 minutes for the highest of his four double centuries in Test matches.

Geoff Marsh was powerless to stop the savage assault by Greenidge and, inevitably, Richie Richardson. Their batting was as spontaneous and uninhibited as the behaviour of the crowd and in just 243 minutes they added 199 in a pure and unforgettable celebration of West Indian cricket before Richardson was dismissed one run shy of his third hundred for the series. He should not, however, have prospered beyond 15 when Merv Hughes ruined Craig McDermott's elaborate plan to entrap him deep behind square leg.

Greenidge, who has long been numbered among the game's most enigmatic champions, played with the ferocious power he has shown ever since he began his career alongside Viv Richards in the Indian garden city of Bangalore in November 1974. Tired of the taunts about his age and angered by suggestions he had lost reflexes and nerve as well as form, he hit out as though there was no tomorrow. Driving and cutting at will against the dispirited attack he enthralled the Barbados crowd with whom he has had an uneasy relationship since he moved to England to play for Hampshire in 1970. On this occasion there was no sign of any resentment from Greenidge or ingratitude from the Bajan fanatics, and he was cheered encouragingly by all when he reached his century with 16 boundaries. There was, however,

Voodoo cricket. Comedian Mac Fingall ceremoniously sprinkling a concoction of his grandmother's intended to buoy the West Indians and curse the Australians. It worked.

much more in store and for the fourth time in his distinguished Test career he converted a hundred to a double century and was mobbed by his more extrovert admirers. At least for 11 hours and 17 minutes he rediscovered the joy of impertinent and impetuous youth and was finally rewarded with 226, his highest Test score and the highest return by a West Indian batsman against Australia.

Indeed, only four older batsmen have scored a double century in Test cricket: South African Eric Rowan (42 years seven days in 1951); the legendary Jack Hobbs (41/196 in 1924); Patsy Hendren (on his 41st birthday in 1930); and South African captain Dudley Nourse (40/208 in 1951).

In a rare display of emotion, the often moody and taciturn Greenidge pointedly raised his bat to spectators all around the ground in what generally was seen as a farewell salute. The crowd rose as one, the older watchers scarcely believing their good fortune at seeing another double century of such magnificence against Australia. In 1954-55 they had the privilege of seeing captain Denis Atkinson return 219 in the astonishing world record seventh wicket stand of 348 with Clairmonte Depeiaza and ten years later had stood for Seymour Nurse when he reached 201 in the same match that Bob Simpson and Bill Lawry each scored double centuries for Australia. Day after day Greenidge's praises were sung privately and publicly. In a letter to the editor of *The Advocate*, Randolph Chase encapsulated the feelings of many Bajans when he composed an ode to Greenidge which began:

Pardon, Gordon,
Oh, pardon
All those who doubted your place.
Now, they can see still intact,
the grace,
the pace,
In the unhurried haste
To 226!

By the time he was adjudged to be leg before wicket to Merv Hughes, Greenidge had lifted the West Indies lead from 15 to a monumental 469. As he withdrew to a salt bath and rubdown table, Viv Richards swaggered to the wicket with the score at 4-454 and the innings 17 minutes into its 12th hour. Although in the annals of Test cricket only India (at Trinidad in 1975-76) and Australia (at Leeds in 1948) have scored more than 400 in a fourth innings of a Test for victory, Richards was loath to declare. He was haunted by the memory of the defeat at Queen's Park Oval in Trinidad five years earlier when Clive Lloyd declared at 6-271 leaving India to score 403 runs in a minimum of 595 minutes. Richards had scored 177 in the first innings and was thunderstruck when India reached 4-406 with seven of the mandatory last 20 overs in hand. Then and there he vowed never to underestimate the supposedly vanquished if he was ever in charge. Only when the lead was a fantastic 551 did Richards finally show mercy and close, so compelling the Australians to survive for 153 overs to save the game they had envisaged winning four days earlier.

Exhausted in body and mind and

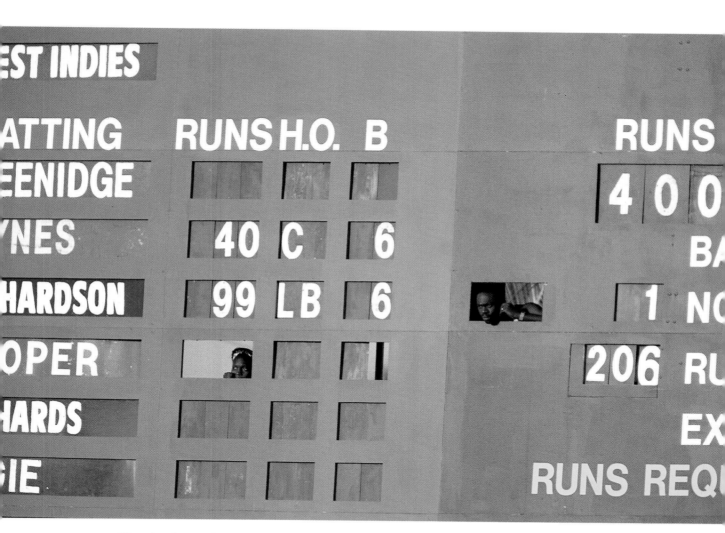

Figuring it out. A scorer and friend survey the scene as Gordon Greenidge, with a little help from his friends, brings the Australians to their knees.

Mark Taylor, Australia's heaviest scoring batsman, makes the characteristic
offering of a left-hander on a pitch offering bounce.

emotionally frayed after 12 hours and 46 minutes in the field the final slide into the abyss began to the first ball of the innings when umpire Lloyd Barker alone considered Marsh leg before wicket to Curtly Ambrose. "Dem going down, down, down, down UNDER," declared one banner. "The crucifixion has begun," said another hastily draped over the railing of the Kensington stand where Mac Fingall continued to cast his proxy spell. To his dismay and consternation the spell somehow was miscast, and over the next three hours the hex fell on the West Indians. Mark Taylor was dropped by Richie Richardson at third slip to Curtly Ambrose, David Boon was bowled by an illegal delivery from Malcolm Marshall and

then dropped by Carl Hooper at second slip to Patrick Patterson. But when Boon played on to a delivery from Curtly Ambrose for 57 the spell returned to its original co-ordinates with a withering force.

Despite the throbbing in his heavily strapped left thumb, the lengthening shadows and the variable bounce of a rapidly wearing pitch Allan Border elected to lead the rearguard action from his customary number four position. While he is well-known for his courage and capacity to play with injury on this occasion he winced in pain from the first ball he played and was unable to hold out against a bowler of the calibre of Ambrose. He edged to wicketkeeper Jeff Dujon the fifth ball he received

High fives squared. Viv Richards takes to the air in excitement as his bowlers move
in for the kill and a precious 2-0 lead in the series.

to record his first duck in 39 innings and only his sixth in 213 innings in 124 Tests. Ambrose, who was also responsible for Border's previous nought, at Melbourne in December 1988, was mobbed by his teammates and the Kensington stand shook to its foundations as Mac Fingall demanded another refrain from the band. Border was the second of four batsmen to record a duck during another innings of breathtaking incompetence — Merv Hughes, Ian Healy and Bruce Reid, for a pair, following suit on the overcast final day.

That the last six wickets fell for 18 runs in 10 overs and 51 minutes compounded the disgrace of the first innings and was an insult to Mark

Taylor who showed exemplary courage and concentration to resist for six hours and eight minutes for 76. In total the Australian batsmen survived for just 10 hours and 54 minutes — 23 minutes less than the world's oldest Test cricketer batted in one innings.

Deliriously excited at a victory by a colossal 343 runs hundreds of spectators spilled on to the ground in front of the Sir Garfield Sobers pavilion to lavish praise on Greenidge and Malcolm Marshall who had so proudly upheld the traditions of Barbados cricket. Greenidge was decorated with the Man of the Match award and Marshall was inducted to a club of such exclusiveness that previously only Sir Richard Hadlee,

159

Ian Botham, Kapil Dev, Imran Khan and Dennis Lillee had gained an introduction. Match figures of 6–95 from 33 overs had taken his aggregate of wickets beyond 350, the prerequisite for admission.

The shock of the humiliation was etched in the faces of the Australians as they sat silently in their dressingroom sedating themselves with beer and loud popular music. Unselfconsciously, Border conducted his post-mortem examination for the Australian press contingent in the ablution alcove. "You've got to give

them credit, they've outplayed us. It is simple as that," he declared with customary candour and graciousness. "I'm not totally distraught, they are a great side."

At a lower level of the pavilion Viv Richards was beaming and smoking a fat cigar in celebration of his second successful defence of the Frank Worrell Trophy. And as was the case at Georgetown he was as relieved as he was satisfied. "There was some element of doubt and people passed on a lot of rhetoric in certain ways. I am very proud, elated for the fact

FOURTH TEST

at Kensington Oval, Bridgetown 19, 20, 21, 23, 24 April — Australia won toss

WEST INDIES

		Min	Balls	4s		Min	Balls	4s
G. Greenidge	c Reid b McDermott	10	42	31	2	lbw b Hughes	226	480	677	32
D. Haynes	c M. Waugh b Hughes	28	212	134	3	c Healy b M. Waugh	40	116	201	3
R. Richardson	c Boon b McDermott	1	10	9	—	lbw b M. Waugh	99	156	243	15
C. Hooper	c Jones b Hughes	0	7	6	—	c Healy b M. Waugh	57	111	184	6
V. Richards	c Hughes b McDermott	32	93	64	6	lbw M. Waugh	25	21	45	4*
G. Logie	c Taylor b Reid	11	42	34	1	not out	33	50	74	5
J. Dujon	c Healy b Hughes	10	26	17	1	c M. Waugh b McDermott	4	13	15	—
M. Marshall	c Marsh b Reid	17	39	33	3	c Healy b McDermott	15	32	60	2
C. Ambrose	not out	19	56	28	3	b Reid	2	5	6	—
C. Walsh	c M. Waugh b McDermott	10	23	20	1	c Marsh b Reid	0	1	1	—
P. Patterson	c M. Waugh b Hughes	1	2	2	—	not out	4	5	15	1
Sundries						Sundries				
(3LB, 7NB)		10				(19LB, 12NB)	31			
Total		149				Nine wickets (dec) for	536			

Fall: 17 (Greenidge), 21 (Richardson), 22 (Hooper), 72 (Richards), 89 (Logie), 96 (Haynes), 103 (Dujon), 125 (Marshall), 148 (Walsh), 149 (Patterson).

Fall: 129 (Haynes), 153 (Marshall), 352 (Richardson), 454 (Greenidge), 470 (Hooper), 512 (Richards), 522 (Dujon), 525 (Ambrose), 525 (Walsh).

	O	M	R	W		O	M	R	W
McDermott	22	7	49	4		37.3	8	130	2
Reid	21	8	50	2		30	4	100	2
Hughes	16.1	2	44	4		36	6	125	1
S. Waugh	2	—	3	—		28	6	77	—
M. Waugh						28	6	80	4
Jones						3	1	5	—

Batting Time: 279 Min. Overs: 61.1

Batting Time: 766 Min. Overs: 162.3
* denotes a six

that the guys shut up a lot of people."

As his press conference progressed it was apparent Richards numbered Bob Simpson among those who should have been silenced by the force of the West Indies performance. Clearly irritated that Simpson had made references to a perceived brittleness in the West Indies batting, Richards said: "I'm not in the business of shouting my mouth off about what we're going to do. I've been hearing what Simpson said the Australians are going to do to us in Australia and before this series. I

don't have great respect for Bob Simpson after seeing the way he operates. I'm not the greatest admirer of Bobby Simpson. You treat people as you are treated."

As he spoke, the Australians, tired, demoralised and painfully aware that the West Indies had never been defeated in Antigua where the final Test was to be played, trudged down the stairs and disappeared into crowded Pickwick Gap. Suddenly they were pretenders to, rather than contenders for, the unofficial championship of the world.

AUSTRALIA

		Min	Balls	4s			Min	Balls	4s
M. Taylor	lbw b Ambrose	26	82	122	2	lbw b Marshall	76	366	243	7
G. Marsh	c Logie b Ambrose	12	31	55	1	lbw b Ambrose	0	1	1	—
D. Boon	c Hooper b Marshall	0	2	4	—	b Ambrose	57	186	135	7
A. Border	b Marshall	29	68	119	4	c Dujon b Ambrose	0	5	8	—
D. Jones	lbw b Marshall	22	51	71	3	b Hooper	37	104	66	6
M. Waugh	not out	20	33	81	3	b Hooper	3	26	27	—
S. Waugh	c Dujon b Patterson	2	5	5	—	not out	4	21	11	—
I. Healy	c Dujon b Walsh	2	10	17	—	lbw b Marshall	0	4	3	—
M. Hughes	c Logie b Walsh	3	15	22	—	c Dujon b Marshall	3	32	28	—
C. McDermott	b Walsh	2	10	11	—	c Sub (Holder) b Walsh	2	10	9	—
B. Reid	b Walsh	0	4	9	—	b Walsh	0	3	1	—
Sundries	(2B, 14NB)		16			Sundries (3B, 5LB, 18NB)	26		
Total			134			Total	208		

Fall: 24 (Marsh), 27 (Boon), 59 (Taylor), 95 (Border), 97 (Jones), 100 (S. Waugh), 106 (Healy), 121 (Hughes), 127 (McDermott), 134 (Reid).

Fall: 0 (Marsh), 111 (Boon), 111 (Border), 122 (Hughes), 190 (Jones), 200 (M. Waugh), 200 (Taylor), 200 (Healy), 208 (McDermott), 208 (Reid).

	O	M	R	W		O	M	R	W
Ambrose	16	5	36	2		19	7	36	3
Patterson	13	6	22	1		15	3	56	—
Marshall	16	1	60	3		17	6	35	3
Walsh	5.1	1	14	4		14.2	3	37	2
Hooper						19	4	28	2
Richards						3	—	8	—

Batting Time: 266 Min. Overs: 50.1

Batting Time: 388 Min. Overs: 87.2

West Indies won by 343 runs

Man of the Match: G. Greenidge. Umpires: L. Barker & D. Archer. 12th Men: T. Alderman (Aust.), B. Lara (W. Ind.).

CHAPTER SIX
THE DIVIDED FIELD

Antigua and the Fifth Test
Recreation Ground • 17 April–1 May 1991

ANTIGUANS WEAR THEIR HEARTS ON
their sleeves and their politics on their chests.
At a restless period in the brief history of the
independent nation of Antigua and Barbuda,
the politics of race, culture and government

Previous pages: Richie Richardson, who succeeded his mentor Viv Richards as the West Indies' principal batsman, at rest in enticing turquoise waters near his village of Five Islands. Above: The sun sets on English Harbour and the flotilla of shining yachts competing at Sailing Week.

dominated the thoughts and actions of the people, particularly the young and impetuous.

With an expediency characteristic of a country living exclusively off the purse of the tourist, the sophisticated, if exploitative, T-shirt industry echoed the mood and concerns of a vast number of the 80 000 people who inhabit the islands.

And with a host of tourists on Antigua for Test cricket and an annual and internationally acclaimed sailing regatta the islanders, at least for a week, could preach to someone other than the converted. From dawn to dusk the politics of the people were paraded along the narrow streets of the unprepossessing capital of St. John's, at the magnificent eighteenth century Nelson's Dockyard at picturesque English Harbour and at

the quaint Recreation Ground with its new Vivian Richards players' pavilion.

While the torso talk provided an appropriately microcosmic view of Antigua which occupies just 279.71 km^2 (108 sq. miles) it also fearlessly addressed issues which stretch far beyond geographical boundaries. Despite the political turmoil within the country, Black consciousness remained the pre-eminent issue. In its racial politics Antigua is closely aligned with Jamaica and the green, gold and red colours of the Rastafari are seen in profusion.

"Black Pioneers" was the maxim on one shirt. "Black heroes in Hall of Fame" shouted another from within a map of Africa divided into horizontal panels of green, gold and red. "Cry

Iconography. American-made cotton and polyester T-shirts extolling the greatness
of "The Antiguan" were eagerly sought by visitors.

Freedom" screamed another. "Mighty Heroes Mandela, Marcus, Martin, Malcolm," observed another with alliterative reference to the distinguished Black leaders Nelson Mandela, Marcus Garvey, Martin Luther King and Malcolm X. But the most visible and provocative and, one sensed, most pertinent, declared: "It's a black thing you wouldn't understand".

Unlike Jamaica, the "One Blood" T-shirt demanding "Let's live together as one or perish together as fools" was conspicuously absent. It was not worn nor was it readily available from any of the innumerable T-shirt stalls throughout the island. Yet, for all their stridency, the young were not without a sense of humour and T-shirts bearing the inscriptions "Rasta Dude Bart Marley" and "New

Age Ganja Turtles" brought a wry smile to the face of the visitor.

Not every slogan and exhortation of the people was silk-screened into nylon, wool and synthetic. There was an increase in political graffiti in St. John's as the government of V. C. Bird, the father of the nation, fought corruption charges and the two weekly newspapers beat the drum in their mastheads. "We stand guard, ensuring progress, truth and justice for all" trumpeted *The Sentinel*. Alongside a photograph of Nelson Mandela, the *Outlet*, the voice of the opposition to the Bird regime, declared that as the "weekly voice of liberation" it was "defending the people's right to know" in "1991 — Freedom From Corruption Year".

That the country was not free from corruption in the highest places was a

165

The reality of life behind the flashy coastal facade catering to the whim of monied tourists. A woman outside a ramshackle house in the street which bears the name of the country's most famous son, Viv Richards.

Cricket crier. Mayfield, a prominent Calypsonian and social commentator, regularly entertained his host of admirers. In dire need of a distraction from happenings in the middle, the crowd revelled in his rivalry with Gravy.

175

Although he was occasionally disconcerted by a steepling delivery, Mark Waugh
graduated with honours to the pinnacle of cricket competition and headed the
Australian averages with 367 runs at 61.17.

so provide the Australians with the impetus to inflict the first defeat on the West Indies at the Recreation Ground. A supremely gifted and versatile cricketer, he had grown in stature as the tour progressed, and as the curtain began to fall on an unremittingly hard series, he produced his *pièce de résistance.* Even against quality pace bowling on a fast and bouncy pitch he had an inordinate amount of time to play his strokes and, as was the case in Adelaide three months earlier, there was an overwhelming sense of inevitability about his hundred.

In Adelaide against England he had become just the 15th Australian to score a century in his Test debut — his 50 coming from 74 balls and his hundred from 126 deliveries with 15 boundaries. Now, in another God-fearing city, he again reached his 50 from 74 balls but this time quickened stride to reach his century from 113 deliveries with nine fours and three sixes. But unlike Adelaide, he did make one blemish offering a return catch to Viv Richards at 97. Such was Waugh's domination of the bowling that the customarily irrepressible Dean Jones was frustrated at being outscored (by 61 to nine) and at 81 played across the line and was leg before wicket to Malcolm Marshall armed with a new ball. Jones had chosen to hit his way out of the doldrums for just his second 50 in 12 Tests and with the rampant Waugh added 186 in 32 overs in a thrilling fifth wicket stand. So slowly did the West Indies bowlers go about their task that the final session lasted 2 hours and 55 minutes and still only

87 overs were bowled for the day. Much as they had done in Jamaica, the Australians pounded the bowlers as they tired, Mark Waugh scoring 110 of the 180 scored between tea and stumps.

The Australian late-order again gave thanks for Mark Waugh but still they did not support him, and in keeping with the inglorious efforts

On song, at last. Out of sorts after a splendid limited-over series, Dean Jones regained form and some confidence with just his second half-century in 12 Tests.

throughout the series the last five wickets fell for 32 runs in 14 overs. Nevertheless, after the unmitigated traumas of Barbados, the capacity to bat for 8 hours and 42 minutes for a score of 403 was good for the soul and balm for the spirit.

Since the maelstrom of Sabina Park, Allan Border was convinced that Craig McDermott bowled as swiftly as any of the feted West Indian fast men and in the prevailing conditions would prove a formidable opponent. And so it proved to be. Incensed that umpire Steve Bucknor refused his leg before wicket appeal against Gordon Greenidge in the solitary over before lunch, McDermott was consumed by resentment and anger. Having refuelled at the smorgasbord he hoed into the elite of the West Indian batting and transfixed the crowd by humbling Richie Richardson and his mentor Viv Richards. Richardson lasted just four balls for three and Richards seven deliveries for nought and the songs of praise to the local heroes, from Nigel "Chickie" Baptiste, the resident disc jockey and impresario, sounded more like a dirge.

Having elicited a positive response from Bucknor against Greenidge at the second attempt, McDermott then aggressively challenged the umpire to rule in his favour on a difficult leg before wicket appeal against Richards. Also an international soccer referee, Bucknor carefully weighed the evidence, shuffled uneasily away from the wicket and then quickly, almost apologetically sent Richards on his way. While Richards had failed against India in 1983 and against England the previous year, Antiguans had not before seen their living deity make a duck. Indeed, in his six innings in the previous five Test matches at the Recreation Ground he had scored 431 runs at an average of 86.2 with two centuries against England and one against Australia. For the only time

at the Test match the crowd fell silent as The Antiguan returned to the pavilion to reflect on his tenth duck in 173 Test innings. His demise did not, however, have any noticeable effect on the sale of the Vivi cologne by Ophir (of London, New York, Toronto and now, Antigua) being sold in gold embossed sachets by voluptuous women wearing the elegant Vivi fragrance T-shirt.

In the middle McDermott continued to sweat, strain and intimidate with the same style of often vicious short-pitched bowling which the Australian batsmen had been consistently subjected to. When he crashed through Desmond Haynes' defence and drew his third affirmative LBW decision from Steve Bucknor, the last line of the West Indian resistance was broken and Curtly Ambrose and Courtney Walsh pooled their resources to avert the follow-on. Haynes, who had played with understandable but uncharacteristic conservatism when things went awry on the first day in Barbados, changed tactics, and with the blatant force of his batting, personality and body language endeavoured to haul the West Indies from the mire. He took 60 of his 84 runs in boundaries, pausing along the way to remonstrate with Merv Hughes who, after the obligatory stare, again found irresistible the urge to respond with a pouted kiss. Meanwhile, Craig McDermott made light of soreness to his left ankle and licked his lips in satisfaction at his return of 4–42 from 15 overs which earned the Australians a handsome lead of 189.

As happened throughout the series,

Madcap Gravy is manhandled by his second after a burlesque stoush with Mayfield.
Gloves were also taken up in the middle but with serious consequences.

peripheral issues deflected attention from heroic deeds in the middle and again there was much huddling and whispering of officials on stairs and in corridors. Despite the best endeavours of the English tabloid press to involve the Australian players in scandal, the most pressing matter before the legislators was the apparently insoluble conflict between Bob Simpson and Viv Richards. Neither party was satisfied with the other's position on a matter which threatened to jeopardise future relations between the administrations, and tensions on the field were duplicated in the boardroom. Neither authority was

prepared to give ground and for days one non-committal statement followed another in an exercise of breathtaking futility. After the umpteenth communiqué, the English Press mockingly issued an "official" statement which, in part, declared: "Following the recent unseemly behaviour of the authorities of the Australian and West Indian cricket boards, the English Press Group wishes to dissociate itself from these two unruly former colonies."

The more provocative of the English scribes were assured of dissociation when they claimed the Australians had broken a lock on the door to their dressingroom and had

Kaleidoscope. The forever changing colours and moods of the animated crowd in the West Indies Oil Co. grandstand.

been ill-mannered when taking food at the smorgasbord. Lawrie Sawle, meanwhile, privately expressed surprise that the Antigua Cricket Association apparently was unfamiliar with the courtesies customarily accorded the manager of a touring team. The ACA also alienated a bevy of photographers from Australia, England and some Caribbean countries by demanding they each pay East Caribbean $500 (A$245) to operate from a prime position behind the bowler's arm adjacent to the pavilion. The fees, it would seem, helped the ACA to defray the cost of cutting away wire meshing in what the "shooters"

termed their snakepit — a cramped space beneath the double-decker grandstand which, each day, became a repository for everything from curried goat to microwaved popcorn. Given the existing mood, the boxing satire enacted by resident comedians Gravy and Mayfield at the tea adjournment was not totally out of context.

Mark Taylor supplanted Mark Waugh as the heaviest scoring Australian batsman for the series when he produced the killer punch against an attack depleted by the absence of the injured Patrick Patterson. Taylor batted for six hours and one minute for 144 to give

Tailpiece. With customary attention to detail Mark Taylor gathered his seventh Test century and was the only Australian to reach 400 runs for the series.

CHICKIE AND THE EGOS

With a flick of a switch at the Recreation Ground, Chickie Baptiste can transform classical cricket theatre into burlesque.

Baptiste has earned a notable reputation as an impresario and up-tempo, up-beat cricket devotees from around the world have joined "Chickie's Posse" since the inaugural Test match in 1981.

Operating from the prime seats in the West Indies Oil Co. grandstand, Chickie presents an unforgettable bash which lasts the duration of the

Good vibrations. Smiling Chickie Baptiste, impresario, disc jockey and bon vivant feels the music while members of his posse dance the day away.

proceedings in the middle. For East Caribbean $200 (A$98) above the match ticket cost of EC$225 (A$110) a cricket-cum-party goer is entitled to an open bar, a substantial lunch each day and a T-shirt which spreads the news of the posse. To boot, the sixty revellers are in front of an imposing bank of speakers and amplifiers and can dance before play, at the fall of a wicket, through each adjournment and into the night. And they do — with gusto.

So loud is the music that vibrations are felt throughout the double-decker stand and even in the adjacent Viv Richards players' pavilion, and all around the ground spectators involuntarily begin to dance when Chickie cues the music.

A professional disc jockey who developed a passion for cricket at Antigua Grammar School, Vivian Richards' alma mater, Chickie ensures the music does not distract the players. He has a library of old and new material to capture the mood of most moments and in 1986 when Richards scored his historic century from fifty-six balls he played the popular song "Captain, the Ship is Sinking" for the benefit of flummoxed England skipper David Gower. When the West Indies duly completed their second consecutive "blackwash" Gower made reference to the ship lying at twenty fathoms.

For the visit of the Australians, Chickie used the popular and catchy promotional theme "Rally 'round the West Indies" for the anthem and at the fall of each wicket aired "Big Stick" with its key lyric: "I'm coming with a stick in my hand".

A trouper at the age of thirty-one, Chickie also provides the accompaniment for the high-camp musical comedy provided by the cross-dressing comic called Gravy and the politically strident Calypsonian known as Mayfield. Indeed, Gravy, be he wearing a tutu, a Santa Claus suit or a pugilist's singlet and trunks, is given to dancing in the most carnal manner atop Chickie's speakers while Mayfield holds court or rocks to and fro on a swing suspended from the rafters of another stand.

In a sense, Chickie is the artistic director of cricket's one theatre of the absurd.

hand. It was ironic that Alderman brought down the curtain for it was his solitary wicket in his only appearance and just his fifth at 94.6 in four Tests on two tours of the Caribbean.

While the Australians regained some confidence and credibility the achievement of inflicting the first defeat on the West Indies at the Recreation Ground was immediately overtaken by wider issues. The relations between the teams had deteriorated to such an extent that Clyde Walcott, the affable president of the West Indies Cricket Board of Control, had no compunction in publicly reprimanding the players as they stood before him like errant schoolboys during the presentation ceremony. Walcott bemoaned the way the series had been played and appealed to the players to mend their ways and respect the game's time-honoured values and virtues. His remarks contrasted starkly from his message in the sponsor Cable and Wireless' tour program, which concluded: "Good luck to both teams and I look forward to all the matches being played in the highest traditions of cricket." It was to such a distressingly bleak backcloth that Mark Taylor was announced the Man of the Match and Richie Richardson, the Man of the Series, was invested with his country's Order of Honour.

At least publicly, Vivian Richards and Allan Border endeavoured to defuse the tension and used the traditional post-match press conference to justify the manner in which the series had been played. Indeed, it seemed as though the skippers were in cahoots.

From the midst of a ruck of tape-toting journalists on the players' viewing balcony Richards declared: "In my case it is a pleasure playing against the Australians because they are a tough sort of unit. We've got a couple of tough guys as well, and when you get two teams as tough as we are you are going to get a few little ill-moments here and there. We've seen that in this particular series but I would like to believe that cricket will always be the survivor. There seems to be bad blood everywhere in cricket today and the game needs to have more respect."

With the blessing of Lloyd Barker, Border repaired to the umpires' cubbyhole in order to be heard above the din of the Australian dressingroom mixed with the bone-jarring finale from Chickie Baptiste's tapedeck and turntable. Border declared: "We were basically determined not to back down. The West Indies are pretty arrogant and aggressive and they have every right to be. They are the best and have been for a long time and we recognise

FIFTH TEST

at Recreation Ground, St. John's 27, 28, 29 April, 1 May — Australia won toss

AUSTRALIA

			Min	Balls	4s		Min	Balls	4s
G. Marsh	c Richards b Patterson	6	17	8	1	c Dujon b Ambrose	1	9	6	—
M. Taylor	c Dujon b Hooper	59	202	123	7	c & b Ambrose	144	361	227	12
D. Boon	c Greenidge b Ambrose	0	17	15	—	b Walsh	35	143	107	2
A. Border	c Dujon b Hooper	59	192	112	8	b Walsh	5	30	36	—
D. Jones	lbw b Marshall	81	188	120	8*	b Walsh	8	18	15	1
M. Waugh	not out	139	307	188	11*	lbw b Walsh	0	1	1	—
I. Healy	c Dujon b Marshall	12	51	41	1	c Logie b Patterson	32	62	43	3
P. Taylor	c Dujon b Ambrose	2	21	18	—	lbw b Marshall	4	41	66	—
M. Hughes	b Ambrose	1	13	11	—	c Walsh b Ambrose	13	33	16	2
C. McDermott	c Dujon b Walsh	7	31	28	—	c Dujon b Marshall	1	13	11	—
T. Alderman	b Walsh	0	4	2	—	not out	0	2	2	—
Sundries	(1B, 12LB, 18NB, 6W)	37				Sundries (11B, 7LB, 4NB)	22			
Total		403				Total	265			

Fall: 10 (Marsh), 13 (Boon), 129 (M. Taylor), 156 (Border), 342 (Jones), 371 (Healy), 381 (P. Taylor), 385 (Hughes), 403 (McDermott), 403 (Alderman).

Fall: 4 (Marsh), 49 (Healy), 142 (Boon), 168 (Border), 184 (Jones), 184 (Waugh), 237 (P. Taylor), 258 (M. Taylor), 265 (Hughes), 265 (McDermott).

	O	M	R	W		O	M	R	W
Ambrose	30	6	92	3		16	1	64	3
Patterson	12	1	44	1		1	—	1	1
Marshall	22	1	72	2		13.1	3	36	2
Walsh	22	1	54	2		26	2	56	4
Hooper	15	2	82	2		27	6	61	—
Richards	7	—	46	—		8	—	29	—

Batting Time: 522 Min. Overs: 108

Batting Time: 386 Min. Overs: 91.1

* denotes six (Waugh 3, Jones 1)

that fact. So we wanted to make sure we didn't back down. When you've got two aggressive sides playing against each other you are going to have clashes. It has been very, very tough. There has been no quarter given in any area and you are always going to have a few skirmishes out in the field under those circumstances. The game is not a waltz in the park any more like the good old days. It's a hard game. And you are going to get clashes. And let's get it right, we are not the only ones who do it."

As the rituals of victory and defeat were enacted in the dressingrooms, Chickie Baptiste and his roadies began to strike the set, the T-shirt sellers closed the window to the souvenir caravan and Gravy, in civvies, held court with admirers. Those drinking beneath the double-decker grandstand at The Pitt Stop, Obsti's, Clarkie's, Kennedy's Bar and Miss Small, Superlady's bar and restaurant, set about apportioning blame both for the result and the ruckus. Sadly, inevitably, the match would be remembered for the wrong reasons.

WEST INDIES

			Min	Balls	4s			Min	Balls	4s
G. Greenidge	lbw b McDermott	6	13	12	—	run out	43	73	115	6*
D. Haynes	lbw b McDermott	84	172	119	15	run out	33	69	94	4
R. Richardson	b McDermott	3	6	4	—	c Jones b Waugh	41	70	79	5*
C. Hooper	lbw b Hughes	2	21	11	—	c Waugh b P. Taylor	35	74	103	2
V. Richards	lbw b McDermott	0	16	7	—	c Alderman b Border	2	8	10	—
G. Logie	c Jones b P. Taylor	24	78	49	3	lbw b Alderman	61	114	176	10
J. Dujon	c Jones b Hughes	33	81	58	2*	lbw b McDermott	4	20	26	—
M. Marshall	c Healy b Waugh	28	69	45	5	lbw b Hughes	51	63	65	5*
C. Ambrose	c M. Taylor b Hughes	8	31	21	1	run out	0	2	2	—
C. Walsh	not out	11	25	15	—	c Healy b Hughes	0	2	2	—
P. Patterson	b Hughes	2	9	6	—	not out	7	6	21	1
Sundries	(2LB, 11NB)	13				Sundries (5B, 7LB, 8NB)	20			
Total		214				Total	297			

Fall: 10 (Greenidge), 22 (Richardson), 35 (Hooper), 46 (Richards), 114 (Logie), 136 (Haynes), 186 (Dujon), 195 (Marshall), 206 (Ambrose), 214 (Patterson).

Fall: 76 (Haynes), 92 (Greenidge), 142 (Richardson), 145 (Richards), 182 (Hooper), 193 (Dujon), 271 (Marshall), 271 (Ambrose), 271 (Walsh), 297 (Logie).

	O	M	R	W		O	M	R	W
McDermott	15	4	42	4		17	2	55	1
Alderman	7	—	42	—		15.4	4	63	1
Hughes	17	2	65	4		19	5	49	2
P. Taylor	11	2	40	1		10	—	39	1
Waugh	5	—	23	1		5	3	8	1
Border						15	2	71	1

Batting Time: 272 Min. Overs: 55

* denotes 2 sixes

Australia won by 157 runs

Batting Time: 365 Min. Overs: 81.4

* denotes six (Greenidge 1, Richardson 1, Marshall 2)

Man of the Match: M. Taylor. Umpires: S. Bucknor & L. Barker. 12th Men: S. Waugh (Aust.), B. Lara (W. Ind.).

West Indies won series 2-1. Man of the Series: R. Richardson

FACT FINDING

AUSTRALIA'S TEST RECORD IN THE CARIBBEAN

	P	W	D	L
1954-55	5	3	2	—
1964-65	5	1	2	2
1972-73	5	2	3	—
1977-78	5	1	1	3
1983-84	5	—	2	3
1990-91	5	1	2	2
Total	30	8	12	10

TEST APPEARANCES
AUSTRALIA V THE WEST INDIES IN THE CARIBBEAN

Australia

Player	
T. Alderman	4
R. Archer	5
J. Benaud	1
R. Benaud	5
D. Boon	5
B. Booth	5
A. Border	10
P. Burge	1
G. Chappell	5
I. Chappell	5
W. Clark	4
G. Cosier	3
R. Cowper	5
R. Darling	3
R. Edwards	5
L. Favell	2
W. Grout	5
N. Harvey	5
J. Hammond	5
N. Hawke	5
I. Healy	5
J. Higgs	4
J. Hill	1
T. Hogan	5
R. Hogg	4
D. Hookes	5
K. Hughes	5
M. Hughes	5
T. Jenner	4
I. Johnson	5
W. Johnston	4
D. Jones	7
G. Langley	4
T. Laughlin	2
W. Lawry	5
G. Lawson	5
D. Lillee	1
R. Lindwall	5
C. McDermott	5
C. McDonald	5
G. McKenzie	5
L. Maddocks	1
J. Maguire	2
G. Marsh	5
R. Marsh	5
G. Matthews	3
L. Mayne	3
K. Miller	5
A. Morris	4
D. Ogilvie	2
K. O'Keefe	5
N. O'Neill	4
W. Phillips	5
P. Philpott	5
C. Rackemann	1
I. Redpath	5
B. Reid	2
G. Ritchie	5
S. Rixon	5
C. Serjeant	5
B. Shepherd	2
R. Simpson	10
D. Sincock	1
S. Smith	3
K. Stackpole	4
M. Taylor	5
P. Taylor	1
G. Thomas	5
J. Thomson	5
P. Toohey	3
M. Walker	5
D. Walters	5
W. Watson	3
M. Waugh	5
S. Waugh	2
K. Wessels	2
M. Whitney	2

G. Wood	6	R. Fredericks	5	D.L. Murray	7
R. Woolley	1	H. Furlonge	1	S. Nurse	4
G. Yallop	4	J. Garner	7	D. Parry	5
B. Yardley	5	G. Gibbs	1	P. Patterson	5
		L. Gibbs	10	N. Phillip	3
West Indies		L. Gomes	5	S. Ramadhin	4
Inshan Ali	3	A. Greenidge	2	V. Richards	12
D. Allan	1	C.G. Greenidge	12	R. Richardson	10
C. Ambrose	5	G.A. Greenidge	3	A. Roberts	2
D. Atkinson	4	C. Griffith	5	W. Rodriguez	1
R. Austin	2	W. Hall	5	L. Rowe	3
S. Bacchus	2	R. Harper	4	S. Shivnarine	3
E. Baptiste	3	D. Haynes	12	I. Shillingford	1
A. Binns	1	J. Hendriks	4	M. Small	1
K. Boyce	4	V. Holder	6	O. Smith	4
B. Butcher	4	M. Holding	3	G. Sobers	9
L. Butler	1	J. Holt	5	J. Solomon	4
S. Clarke	1	C. Hooper	5	J. Stollmeyer	2
C. Croft	2	C. Hunte	5	A. Valentine	3
W. Daniel	2	R. Jumadeen	3	C. Walcott	5
B. Davis	4	A. Kallicharran	10	C. Walsh	5
C. Davis	2	R. Kanhai	10	E. Weekes	5
W. Davis	1	F. King	4	A. White	2
C. Depeiza	3	C. Lloyd	9	E. Willett	3
T. Dewdney	2	G. Logie	6	A. Williams	3
U. Dowe	1	C. McWatt	1	F. Worrell	4
J. Dujon	10	M. Marshall	9		
T. Findlay	1	N. Marshall	1		
M. Foster	5	D.A. Murray	3		

Highest Innings Totals

Australia	758-8d	Kingston	1954-55
West Indies	573	Bridgetown	1964-65

Lowest Innings Totals

Australia	90	Port of Spain	1977-78
West Indies	109	Georgetown	1972-73

Highest Aggregate of Runs in a Series

Australia	N. Harvey	650 (Av. 108.33)	1954-55
West Indies	C. Walcott	827 (Av. 82.70)	1954-55

Highest Aggregate Wickets in a Series

Australia	M. Walker	26 (Av. 20.73)	1972-73
West Indies	J. Garner	31 (Av. 16.87)	1983-84

Carried Bat

West Indies	C. Hunte 60* out of 131	Port of Spain	1964-65

Failure to Score in Each Innings of a Test

Australia	W. Clark	Port of Spain	1977-78
	W. Clark	Bridgetown	1977-78
	B. Reid	Bridgetown	1990-91
West Indies	A. Binns	Kingston	1954-55
	O. Smith	Port of Spain	1954-55

Centuries
Australia

R. Archer	128	Kingston	1954-55
R. Benaud	121	Kingston	1954-55
D. Boon	109*	Kingston	1990-91
B. Booth	117	Port of Spain	1964-65
A. Border	100*	Port of Spain	1983-84
G. Chappell	106	Bridgetown	1972-73
I. Chappell	106*	Bridgetown	1972-73
	109	Georgetown	1972-73
R. Cowper	143	Port of Spain	1964-65
	102	Bridgetown	1964-65
N. Harvey	133	Kingston	1954-55
	133	Port of Spain	1954-55
	204	Kingston	1954-55
W. Lawry	210	Bridgetown	1964-65
R. Lindwall	118	Bridgetown	1954-55
C. McDonald	110	Port of Spain	1954-55
	127	Kingston	1954-55
K. Miller	147	Kingston	1954-55
	137	Bridgetown	1954-55
	109	Kingston	1954-55
A. Morris	111	Port of Spain	1954-55
W. Phillips	120	Bridgetown	1983-84
C. Serjeant	124	Georgetown	1977-78
R. Simpson	201	Bridgetown	1964-65
K. Stackpole	142	Kingston	1972-73
M. Taylor	144	St. John's	1990-91
P. Toohey	122	Kingston	1977-78

D. Walters	102*	Bridgetown	1972-73
	112	Port of Spain	1972-73
M. Waugh	139	St. John's	1990-91
G. Wood	126	Georgetown	1977-78

West Indies

D. Atkinson	219	Bridgetown	1954-55
B. Butcher	117	Port of Spain	1964-65
C. Depeiza	122	Bridgetown	1954-55
J. Dujon	130	Port of Spain	1983-84
M. Foster	125¶	Kingston	1972-73
L. Gomes	101¶	Georgetown	1977-78
	115	Kingston	1977-78
C.G. Greenidge	120*	Georgetown	1983-84
	127	Kingston	1983-84
	226	Bridgetown	1990-91
D. Haynes	103*	Georgetown	1983-84
	145	Bridgetown	1983-84
	111	Georgetown	1990-91
A. Kallicharran	127	Port of Spain	1977-78
	126	Kingston	1977-78
R. Kanhai	129	Bridgetown	1964-65
	121	Port of Spain	1964-65
	105	Bridgetown	1972-73
C. Lloyd	178	Georgetown	1972-73
S. Nurse	201	Bridgetown	1964-65
V. Richards	178	St. John's	1983-84
R. Richardson	131*	Bridgetown	1983-84
	154	St. John's	1983-84
	104*	Kingston	1990-91
	182	Georgetown	1990-91
O. Smith	104¶	Kingston	1954-55
C. Walcott	108	Kingston	1954-55
	126#	Port of Spain	1954-55
	110#	Port of Spain	1954-55
	155#	Kingston	1954-55
	110#	Kingston	1954-55
E. Weekes	139	Port of Spain	1954-55
A. Williams	100¶	Georgetown	1977-78

\# denotes century in each innings of Test

¶ denotes century on debut

* denotes not out

Ten or more Wickets in a Match
Australia

| N. Hawke | 10/115 | Georgetown | 1964-65 |

AUSTRALIA IN THE WEST INDIES: RESULTS

Venue	Result	Australia		West Indies		Captains	
1954-55							
Kingston	Australia 9 wickets	o515-9d	20-1	259	295		D. Atkinson
Port of Spain	Drawn	600-9d	—	o382	273-4		J. Stollmeyer
Georgetown	Australia 8 wickets	257	133-2	o182	207	I. Johnson	J. Stollmeyer
Bridgetown	Drawn	o668	249	510	234-6		D. Atkinson
Kingston	Australia Inns & 82 runs	758-8d	—	o357	319		D. Atkinson
1964-65							
Kingston	West Indies 179 runs	217	216	o239	373		
Port of Spain	Drawn	516	—	o429	386		
Georgetown	West Indies 212 runs	179	144	o355	180	R. Simpson	G. Sobers
Bridgetown	Drawn	o650-6d	174-4d	573	242-5		
Port of Spain	Australia 10 wickets	294	63-0	o224	131		
1972-73							
Kingston	Drawn	o428-7d	260-2d	428	67-3		
Bridgetown	Drawn	o324	300-2d	391	36-0		
Port of Spain	Australia 44 runs	o332	281	280	289	I. Chappell	R. Kanhai
Georgetown	Australia 10 wickets	341	135-0	o366	109		
Port of Spain	Drawn	o419-8d	218-7d	319	135-5		
1977-78							
Port of Spain	West Indies Inns & 106 runs	o 90	209	405	—		C. Lloyd
Bridgetown	West Indies 9 wickets	o250	178	288	141-1		C. Lloyd
Georgetown	Australia 3 wickets	286	362-7	o205	290	R. Simpson	A. Kallicharran
Port of Spain	West Indies 198 runs	290	94	o292	290		A. Kallicharran
Kingston	Drawn	o343	305-3d	280	258-9		A. Kallicharran

1983-84

Venue					Result	Australia	West Indies
Georgetown	o279	273-9d	230	250-0	Drawn		C. Lloyd
Port of Spain	o255	299-9	468-8d	—	Drawn		V. Richards
Bridgetown	o429	97	509	21-0	West Indies 10 wickets	K. Hughes	C. Lloyd
St. John's	o262	200	498	—	West Indies Inns & 36 runs		C. Lloyd
Kingston	o199	160	305	55-0	West Indies 10 wickets		C. Lloyd

1990-91

Venue					Result	Australia	West Indies
Kingston	371	—	o264	334-3	Drawn		
Georgetown	o348	248	569	31-0	West Indies 10 wickets		
Port of Spain	o294	123-3	227	—	Drawn	A. Border	V. Richards
Bridgetown	134	208	o149	536-9d	West Indies 343 runs		
St. John's	o403	265	214	297	Australia 157 runs		

o denotes batted first

AUSTRALIA IN THE WEST INDIES: RESULTS IN SUMMARY

	Tests	Results			Kingston			Port of Spain			Georgetown			Bridgetown			St. John's		
		A	W1	D	A	W1	D	A	W1	D	A	W1	D	A	W1	D	A	W1	D
1954-55	5	3	—	2	2	—	—	—	—	1	1	—	—	—	—	1	—	—	—
1964-65	5	1	2	2	—	1	—	1	—	1	—	1	—	—	—	1	—	—	—
1972-73	5	2	—	3	—	—	1	1	—	1	1	—	—	—	—	1	—	—	—
1977-78	5	1	3	1	—	—	1	—	2	—	1	—	—	—	1	—	—	—	—
1983-84	5	—	3	2	—	1	—	—	—	1	—	—	1	—	1	—	—	1	—
1990-91	5	1	2	2	—	—	1	—	—	1	—	1	—	—	1	—	1	—	—
Totals	30	8	10	12	2	2	3	2	2	5	3	2	1	—	3	3	1	1	—

1991 TEST AVERAGES

Australia Batting

	M	Inns	NO	HS	Agg	Average	Catches
M. Waugh	5	8	2	139*	367	61.17	10
M. Taylor	5	9	—	144	441	49.00	3
A. Border	5	9	1	59	275	34.38	1
D. Boon	5	9	1	109*	266	33.25	1
D. Jones	5	9	1	81	245	30.63	4
G. Marsh	5	9	—	94	226	25.11	4
I. Healy	5	8	—	53	155	19.38	10
S. Waugh	2	3	1	26	32	16.00	1
G. Matthews	2	3	—	16	27	9.00	—
M. Hughes	5	8	—	21	41	5.13	2
P. Taylor	1	2	—	4	6	3.00	—
M. Whitney	2	3	2	2	3	3.00	—
C. McDermott	5	8	—	7	18	2.25	2
T. Alderman	1	2	1	0*	0	0.00	1
B. Reid	2	3	1	0*	0	0.00	1

*denotes not out

Australia Bowling

	Overs	Maidens	Runs	Wickets	Average
M. Waugh	65	18	183	8	22.88
C. McDermott	192.5	40	564	24	23.50
A. Border	54	21	188	7	26.86
M. Hughes	172.3	32	589	19	31.00
P. Taylor	21	2	79	2	39.50
B. Reid	73	12	229	5	45.80
G. Matthews	73.5	10	273	3	91.00
T. Alderman	22.4	4	105	1	105.00
M. Whitney	66	11	216	—	—
S. Waugh	35	6	90	—	—
D. Jones	4	1	9	—	—

West Indies Batting

	M	Inns	NO	HS	Agg	Average	Catches
R. Richardson	5	8	1	182	475	67.86	1
G. Logie	5	7	2	77*	261	52.20	4
D. Haynes	5	9	1	111	412	51.50	—
G. Greenidge	5	9	1	226	366	45.75	1
J. Dujon	5	7	—	70	209	29.86	23
C. Hooper	5	8	—	62	199	24.88	7
V. Richards	5	8	1	52*	174	24.86	1
M. Marshall	5	7	1	51	145	24.17	—
C. Ambrose	5	7	1	53	115	19.17	1
C. Walsh	5	7	2	12*	44	8.80	2
P. Patterson	5	7	2	15	33	6.60	1

*denotes not out

West Indies Bowling

	Overs	Maidens	Runs	Wickets	Average
M. Marshall	156.2	25	437	21	20.81
P. Patterson	136	19	409	18	22.72
C. Walsh	179.3	32	426	17	25.06
C. Ambrose	205.4	47	493	18	27.39
C. Hooper	151	37	391	5	78.20
V. Richards	23	2	101	—	—
R. Richardson	1	—	2	—	—

CALYPSO CLIPS

- Bruce Yardley was called for throwing by Umpire Douglas Sang Hue during the Australians' match against Jamaica in 1977-78.

- Clive Walcott (1954–55 series) is the only batsman in Test history to hit centuries in both innings of a Test twice in the one series. Walcott's five centuries in that series is also a world record.

- Richie Benaud's century in 78 minutes at Kingston in 1954-55 is the fastest in Australia–West Indies clashes.

- Denis Atkinson and Clairmonte Depeiza's 7th wicket stand of 347 at Bridgetown in 1954-55 still stands as a world record. Depeiza's 122 was his only century in first class cricket.

- Doug Walters scored a hundred runs in a session during his innings of 112 at Port of Spain in 1972-73.

- The opening stand of 382 by Bob Simpson and Bill Lawry at Barbados in 1964-65 is a record for Australia in all Tests.

- The final Test at Kingston in 1977-78 could not be finished after crowd riots. The match was rescheduled into a sixth day but abandoned when the umpires declined to officiate.

- Bob Simpson was 42 years and 19 days old when he played his first one-day international at St. John's, Antigua on 22 February 1978.

- The 21 hundreds scored in 1954–55 is a record for a Five-Test series. Australia scored 12 and the West Indies nine.

THIRD LIMITED OVERS INTERNATIONAL

at Queen's Park Oval, Port of Spain 10 March — Australia won toss

AUSTRALIA

G. Marsh	b Gray	81
M. Taylor	c Haynes b Ambrose	3
D. Jones	c Richards b Gray	36
M. Waugh	b Simmons	17
A. Border	c Dujon b Patterson	22
S. Waugh	b Ambrose	23
I. Healy	not out	33
P. Taylor	b Ambrose	2
C. McDermott	not out	3
Sundries	(2B, 10LB, 4NB, 9W)	25
	Seven wickets for	245

Fall: 13, 82, 116, 165, 191, 225, 239.

B. Reid & M. Whitney did not bat.

	O	M	R	W
Ambrose	10	1	37	3
Patterson	9	—	52	1
Gray	10	—	59	2
Simmons	10	—	35	1
Hooper	10	—	50	—

WEST INDIES

P. Simmons	c Healy b Reid	0
D. Haynes	b S. Waugh	16
R. Richardson	c Border b M. Waugh	90
G. Greenidge	not out	40
G. Logie	not out	24
Sundries	(1B, 5LB, 2NB, 3W)	11
	Three wickets for	181

Fall: 3, 72, 132.

C. Ambrose, J. Dujon, A. Gray, C. Hooper, P. Patterson & V. Richards did not bat.

	O	M	R	W
Reid	7	—	28	1
McDermott	5	—	21	—
S. Waugh	7	—	39	1
P. Taylor	2	—	17	—
Whitney	7	—	38	—
M. Waugh	5.3	—	32	1

West Indies won on superior run rate. Man of the Match: R. Richardson. Umpires: C. Cumberbatch & L. Barker.

FOURTH LIMITED OVERS INTERNATIONAL

at Kensington Oval, Bridgetown 13 March — Australia won toss

AUSTRALIA

M. Taylor	c Dujon b Ambrose	5
G. Marsh	b Ambrose	113
D. Jones	c Walsh b Marshall	7
A. Border	c Ambrose b Hooper	79
M. Waugh	run out	49
S. Waugh	lbw b Ambrose	5
I. Healy	not out	6
C. McDermott	not out	1
Sundries	(2B, 7LB, 5NB, 4W)	18
	Six wickets for	283

Fall: 19, 27, 173, 260, 271, 276.

P. Taylor, B. Reid & M. Whitney did not bat.

	O	M	R	W
Ambrose	10	1	38	3
Marshall	10	1	67	1
Walsh	10	—	46	—
Simmons	6	—	37	—
Richards	4	—	29	—
Hooper	10	—	57	1

WEST INDIES

P. Simmons	b McDermott	23
D. Haynes	b Reid	22
R. Richardson	c McDermott b Whitney	25
G. Greenidge	lbw b S. Waugh	17
V. Richards	c & b S. Waugh	20
G. Logie	c M. Taylor b M. Waugh	37
C. Hooper	c M. Waugh b P. Taylor	18
J. Dujon	c P. Taylor b M. Waugh	39
M. Marshall	c Whitney b McDermott	19
C. Ambrose	not out	12
C. Walsh	c & b M. Waugh	4
Sundries	(6LB, 3NB, 1W)	10
Total		246

Fall: 39, 49, 89, 95, 118, 158, 177, 226, 241, 246.

	O	M	R	W
Reid	7	—	52	1
McDermott	8	—	40	2
S. Waugh	7	—	25	2
Whitney	10	1	39	1
P. Taylor	8	—	50	1
M. Waugh	7	—	34	3

Australia won by 37 runs. Man of the Match: G. Marsh. Umpires: D. Archer & L. Barker.

FIFTH LIMITED OVERS INTERNATIONAL

at Bourda, Georgetown 20 March — West Indies won toss

WEST INDIES

P. Simmons	c Hughes b Taylor	34
D. Haynes	lbw b Taylor	58
R. Richardson	c Healy b Hughes	94
G. Greenidge	run out	6
V. Richards	c Whitney b M. Waugh	10
G. Logie	b McDermott	17
C. Hooper	c Taylor b McDermott	10
J. Dujon	b Hughes	2
A. Gray	c Border b McDermott	6
C. Walsh	b Hughes	2
P. Patterson	not out	1
Sundries	(8LB, 2NB, 1W)	11
Total		251

Fall: 85, 115, 136, 155, 217, 237, 239, 246, 248, 251.

	O	M	R	W
McDermott	10	—	29	3
Hughes	9.5	—	33	3
S. Waugh	3	—	33	—
Whitney	9	—	46	—
Taylor	10	—	45	2
M. Waugh	6	—	36	1
Border	2	—	21	—

AUSTRALIA

G. Marsh	not out	106
D. Boon	b Patterson	9
D. Jones	run out	11
A. Border	c Dujon b Walsh	60
M. Waugh	st Dujon b Hooper	7
S. Waugh	not out	26
Sundries	(4B, 4LB, 14NB, 11W)	33
Four wickets for		252

Fall: 12, 37, 161, 181.

I. Healy, M. Hughes, C. McDermott, P. Taylor & M. Whitney did not bat.

	O	M	R	W
Patterson	6.3	—	34	1
Gray	8	—	44	—
Walsh	10	—	54	1
Simmons	10	—	53	—
Hooper	10	—	45	1
Richards	4	—	14	—

Australia won by six wickets. Man of the Match: G. Marsh. Umpires: C. Cumberbatch & C. Duncan. Australia won series 4-1.

INDEX

Page numbers in italic refer to photographs.